11.50

STUDIES IN ECONOMICS AND POLITICAL SCIENCE

Edited by

THE DIRECTOR OF THE LONDON SCHOOL OF ECONOMICS
AND POLITICAL SCIENCE

No. 107 in the series of Monographs by writers connected with the
London School of Economics and Political Science

PRICES AND PRODUCTION

PRICES AND PRODUCTION

BY

FRIEDRICH A. HAYEK

AUGUSTUS M. KELLEY, *Publishers*
NEW YORK

First published September 1931
Reprinted January 1932
Second edition (revised and enlarged) 1935
Reprinted 1941, 1946, 1949, 1951, 1957, 1960 *and* 1967

Published in the U.S.A. by Augustus M. Kelly, Publishers
New York

Library of Congress Catalogue Number
67-19586

Printed in Great Britain

CONTENTS

▼

PREFACE TO THE SECOND EDITION

THIS book owes its existence to an invitation by the University of London to deliver during the session 1930-31 four lectures to advanced students in economics, and in the form in which it was first published it literally reproduced these lectures. This invitation offered to me what might easily have been a unique opportunity to lay before an English audience what contribution I thought I had then to make to current discussions of theoretical economics ; and it came at a time when I had arrived at a clear view of the outlines of a theory of industrial fluctuations but before I had elaborated it in full detail or even realised all the difficulties which such an elaboration presented. The exposition, moreover, was limited to what I could say in four lectures, which inevitably led to even greater oversimplification than I would probably have been guilty of in any other case. But although I am now conscious of many more defects of this exposition than I was even at the time of its first publication, I can only feel profoundly grateful to the circumstances which were such an irresistible temptation to publish these ideas at an earlier date than I should otherwise have done. From the criticisms and discussions that publication has caused I hope to have profited more for a later more complete exposition than I could possibly have done if I had simply continued to work on these problems for myself.   But the time for that more exhaustive treatment of these problems has not yet come.   It is perhaps the main gain which I derived from the early publication that it made it clear to me that before I could hope to get much further with the elucidation of the main problems discussed in this book it would be necessary considerably to elaborate the foundations on which I have tried to build.   Contact with scientific circles which were less inclined than I was to take for granted the main propositions of the " Austrian " theory of capital on which I have drawn so freely in this book has shown—not that these propositions were wrong or that they were less important than I had thought for the task for which I had used them—but that they would have to be developed in far greater detail and have to be adapted much more closely to the complicated conditions of real life before they could provide a completely satisfactory instrument for the explanation of the particularly complicated phenomena to which I have applied them. This is a task which has to be undertaken before the theses expounded in the present book can be developed further with advantage.

Under these circumstances, when a new edition of this book was called for, I felt neither prepared to rewrite and enlarge it to the extent that a completely adequate treatment of the problems taken up would make necessary, nor to see it reappear in an altogether unchanged form.   The compression of the original exposition has given rise to so many unnecessary misunderstandings which a somewhat fuller treatment would have prevented that certain additions seemed urgently necessary. I have accordingly chosen the middle course of inserting into the, on the whole unchanged, original text further elucidations and elaborations where they seemed most necessary. Many of these additions were already included in the German edition which appeared a few months after the first English edition. Others are taken over from a number of articles in which in the course of the last three years I have tried to develop or to defend the main thesis of this book. It has, however, been by no means possible to incorporate all the further elaborations attempted in these articles in the present volume and the reader who may wish to refer to them will find them listed in the footnote below.[1]

By these modifications I hope to have removed at least some of the difficulties which the book seems to have presented in its original form. Others were due to the fact that the book was in some ways a continuation of an argument which I had begun in other publications that at the time of its first appearance were available only in German. In the meantime English

---

[1] " The Pure Theory of Money, A Rejoinder to Mr. Keynes ", *Economica*, November, 1931 ; " Money and Capital, A Reply to Mr. Sraffa ", *Economic Journal*, June, 1932 ; " Kapitalaufzehrung ", *Weltwirtschaftliches Archiv*, July, 1932 ; " A Note on the Development of the Doctrine of ' Forced Saving '," *Quarterly Journal of Economics*, November, 1932 ; *Der Stand und dei nächste Zukunft der Konjunkturforschung*, Festschrift für Arthur Spiethoff, München, 1933 ; " Ueber neutrales Geld ", *Zeitschrift für Nationalökonomie*, vol. IV, October, 1933 ; " Capital and Industrial Fluctuations ", *Econometrica*, vol. II, April, 1934 ; " On the Relationship between Investment and Output ", *Economic Journal*, June, 1934.

translations have, however, been published[1] and in those the reader will find explained some of the assumptions which are implicit rather than explicitly stated in the following discussion.

Some of the real difficulties which I fully realise this book must present to most readers will, however, not be removed by either of these changes because they are inherent in the mode of exposition adopted. All I can do in this respect short of replacing this book by an entirely new one is to draw the attention of the reader in advance to this particular difficulty and to explain why the mode of exposition which causes it had to be adopted.   This is all the more necessary since this irremediable defect of the exposition has caused more misunderstandings than any other single problem.

The point in question is shortly this.   Considerations of time made it necessary for me in these lectures to treat at one and the same time the real changes of the structure of production which accompany changes in the amount of capital and the monetary mechanism which brings this change about.   This was possible only under highly simplified assumptions which made any change in the monetary demand for capital goods proportional to the change in the total demand for capital goods which it brought about.   Now "demand" for capital goods, in the sense in which it can be said that demand determines their value, of course does not consist exclusively or even primarily in a demand exercised on any market,

---

[1] *Monetary Theory and the Trade Cycle*, London, 1933 ; " The Paradox of Saving ", *Economica*, May, 1931.

but to a perhaps even greater degree in a demand or willingness to continue to hold capital goods for a further period of time. On the relationship between this total demand and the monetary demand for capital goods which manifests itself on the markets during any period of time, no general statements can be made ; nor is it particularly relevant for my problems what this quantitative relationship actually is. What was, however, of prime importance for my purpose was to emphasise that any change in the monetary demand for capital goods could not be treated as something which made itself felt only on some isolated market for new capital goods, but that it could be only understood as a change affecting the general demand for capital goods which is an essential aspect of the process of maintaining a given structure of production. The simplest assumption of this kind which I could make was to assume a fixed relationship between the monetary and the total demand for capital goods so as to make the amount of money spent on capital goods during a unit period of time equal to the value of the stock of capital goods in existence.

This assumption, which I still think is very useful for my main purpose, proved however to be somewhat misleading in two other, not unimportant, respects. In the first instance it made it impossible to treat adequately the case of durable goods. It is impossible to assume that the potential services, embodied in a durable good and waiting for the moment when they will be utilised, change hands at regular intervals of time. This meant that so far as that particular illustration of the monetary mechanism was concerned I had to leave durable goods simply out of account. I did not feel that this was too serious a defect, particularly as I was under the—I think not unjustified—impression that the rôle which circulating capital played was rather neglected and accordingly wanted to stress it as compared with that of fixed capital. But I realise now that I should have given proper warning of the exact reason why I introduced this assumption and what function it performed, and I am afraid that the footnote which I inserted in the first edition (page 37, note 2) at the last moment, when my attention was drawn to the difficulty which my argument might present, has served rather to confuse than to clear up the point.

The second effect of this assumption of separate " stages " of production of equal length was that it imposed upon me a somewhat one-sided treatment of the problem of the velocity of circulation of money. It implied more or less that money passed through the successive stages at a constant rate which corresponded to the rate at which the goods advanced through the process of production, and in any case excluded considerations of changes in the velocity of circulation or the cash balances held in the different stages. The impossibility of dealing expressly with changes in the velocity of circulation so long as this assumption was maintained served to strengthen the misleading impression that the phenomena I was discussing would be caused only by actual changes in the quality of money and not by every change in the money stream, which in the real world are probably caused at least as frequently, if not more frequently, by changes in the velocity of circulation than by changes in the actual quantity. It has been put to me that any treatment of monetary problems which neglected in this way the phenomenon of changes in the desire to hold money balances could not possibly say anything worthwhile. While in my opinion this is a somewhat exaggerated view, I should like to emphasise in this connection how small a section of the whole field of monetary theory is actually treated in this book. All that I claim for it is that it deals with an aspect which has been more neglected and misunderstood than perhaps any other and the insufficient understanding of which has led to particularly serious mistakes. To incorporate this argument into the body of monetary theory is a task which has yet to be undertaken and which I could not and did not try to undertake here. But I may perhaps add that so far as the general theory of money (as distinguished from the pure theory of capital) is concerned, it is the work of Professor Mises[1] much more than that of Knut Wicksell which provides the framework inside which I have tried to elaborate a special point.

[1] See particularly his *Theorie des Geldes und der Umlaufsmittel*, first published in 1912 and now fortunately available in an English translation: L. Mises, *The Theory of Money*, London (Jonathan Cape), 1934. *Cf.* also my *Monetary Theory and the Trade Cycle*, London 1933, which is concerned more with the monetary factors which *cause* the trade cycle than the present book which is mainly devoted to the real phenomena which constitute it.

In addition to this acknowledgment of a great intellectual obligation I should like to repeat from the Preface to the first edition not only the acknowledgment of what I owe to the great tradition in the field of the theory of capital which is connected with the names of W. S. Jevons, E. v. Böhm-Bawerk and K. Wicksell, but also of the more specific debt to those who have helped me in the preparation of these lectures : to Mr. Albert G. Hart, now of the University of Chicago, who gave me the benefit of his advice when I was drafting the original English manuscript of these lectures and particularly to Professor Lionel Robbins, who, when the first edition was published, undertook the considerable labour of putting the manuscript into a form fit for publication and seeing it through the press, and who ever since has most generously given me his help with all my English publications, including the present second edition of this book.

F. A. v. HAYEK.

The London School of Economics
      and Political Science.

August, 1934.

LECTURE I

THEORIES OF THE INFLUENCE OF MONEY ON PRICES

" He realised well that the abundance of money makes everything dear, but he did not analyse how that takes place. The great difficulty of this analysis consists in discovering by what path and in what proportion the increase of money raises the price of things."

RICHARD CANTILLON (died 1734),
Essai sur la nature du commerce en général, II, 6.

(1) THAT monetary influences play a dominant rôle in determining both the volume and direction of production is a truth which is probably more familiar to the present generation than to any which have gone before. The experiences of the war- and post-war-inflation, and of the return to the gold standard, particularly where, as in Great Britain, it was accomplished by a contraction of the circulation, have given abundant evidence of the dependence on money of every productive activity. The widespread discussions of recent years concerning the desirability and practicability of stabilising the value of money, are due mainly to a general recognition of this fact. At the present moment many of the best minds believe the cause of the existing world-wide depression to be a scarcity of gold and seek accordingly for monetary means to overcome it.

And yet, if it were asked whether understanding of the connection between money and prices has made great progress during these years, at any rate until very recently, or whether the generally accepted doctrines on this point have progressed far beyond what was generally known a hundred years ago, I should be inclined to answer in the negative. This may seem paradoxical, but I think anyone who has studied the monetary literature of the first half of the nineteenth century will agree that there is hardly any idea in contemporary monetary theory which was not known to one or more writers of that period. Probably the majority of present-day economists would contend that the reason why progress has been so slight is that monetary theory has already reached such a state of perfection that further progress must of necessity be slow. But I confess that to me it still seems that some of the most fundamental problems in this field remain unsolved, that some of the accepted doctrines are of a very doubtful validity, and that we have even failed to develop the suggestions for improvement which can be found in the works of these early writers.

If that be true, and I hope to convince you that it is, it is surely somewhat astonishing that the experiences of the last fifteen years have not proved more fruitful. In the past, periods of monetary disturbance have always been periods of great progress in this branch of Economics. The Italy of the sixteenth century has been called the country of the worst money and the best monetary theory. If recently that has not been true to the same extent, the reason seems to me to lie in a certain change of attitude on the part of most economists in regard to the appropriate methodology of economics, a change which in many quarters is hailed as a great progress : I mean the attempt to substitute quantitative for qualitative methods of investigation. In the field of monetary theory, this change has been made even by economists who in general reject the " new " point of view, and indeed several had made it some years before the quantitative method had become fashionable elsewhere.

(2) The best known instance, and the most relevant case in point, is the resuscitation by Irving Fisher some twenty years ago of the more mechanistic forms of the quantity theory of the value of money in his well-known " equation of exchange ". That this theory, with its apparatus of mathematical formulæ constructed to admit of statistical verification, is a typical instance of " quantitative " economics, and that it indeed probably contributed a good deal to influence the methodology of the present representatives of this school, are propositions which are not likely to be denied. I do not propose to quarrel with the positive content of this theory : I am even ready to concede that so far as it goes it is true, and that, from a practical point of view, it would be one of the worst things which would befall us if the general public should ever again cease to believe in the elementary propositions of the quantity theory. What I complain of is not only that this theory in its various forms has unduly

usurped the central place in monetary theory, but that the point of view from which it springs is a positive hindrance to further progress. Not the least harmful effect of this particular theory is the present isolation of the theory of money from the main body of general economic theory.

For so long as we use different methods for the explanation of values as they are supposed to exist irrespective of any influence of money, and for the explanation of that influence of money on prices, it can never be otherwise. Yet we are doing nothing less than this if we try to establish *direct* causal connections between the *total* quantity of money, the *general level* of all prices and, perhaps, also the *total* amount of production. For none of these magnitudes *as such* ever exerts an influence on the decisions of individuals; yet it is on the assumption of a knowledge of the decisions of individuals that the main propositions of non-monetary economic theory are based. It is to this " individualistic " method that we owe whatever understanding of economic phenomena we possess; that the modern " subjective " theory has advanced beyond the classical school in its consistent use is probably its main advantage over their teaching.

If, therefore, monetary theory still attempts to establish causal relations between aggregates or general averages, this means that monetary theory lags behind the development of economics in general. In fact, neither aggregates nor averages do act upon one another, and it will never be possible to establish necessary connections of cause and effect between them as we can between individual phenomena, individual prices, etc. I would even go so far as to assert that, from the very nature of economic theory, averages can never form a link in its reasoning; but to prove this contention would go far beyond the subject of these lectures. I shall here confine myself to an attempt to show in a special field the differences between explanations which do and explanations which do not have recourse to such concepts.

(3) As I have said already, I do not want to criticise the doctrines of these theories so far as they go; I indicate their characteristics only in order to be able to show later on how much more another type of theory may accomplish. The central preoccupation of these theories is changes in the general price level. Now everybody agrees that a change of prices would be of no consequence whatever if all prices in the widest sense of the term were affected equally and simultaneously. But the main concern of this type of theory is avowedly, with certain suppositions " tendencies, which affect *all* prices equally, or at any rate impartially, at the same time and in the same direction ".[1] And it is only after the alleged causal relation between changes in the quantity of money and average prices has thus been established that effects on relative prices are considered. But as the assumption generally is that changes in the quantity of money affect only the general

[1] This is the formulation of R. G. Hawtrey. *Cf.* his lecture on " Money and Index Numbers " in the *Journal of the Royal Statistical Society*, Vol. XCIII, Part I, 1930, p. 65.

price level, and that changes of relative prices are due to " disturbing factors " or "frictions", changes in relative prices are not part of this explanation of the changes in the price level. They are mere accompanying circumstances which experience has taught us to be regularly connected with changes of the price level, not, as might be thought, necessary consequences of the same causes. This is very clear from the form of exposition and the concepts it employs. Certain " lags " are found to exist between the changes of different prices. The prices of different goods are said generally to be affected in a definite sequence, and it is always implied that all this would never take place if the general price level did not change.

When we come to the way in which the influence of prices on production is conceived by this theory, the same general characteristics are to be discovered. It is the price level, the changes of which are supposed to influence production ; and the effect considered is not the effect upon particular branches of production, but the effect upon the volume of production in general. In most cases, no attempt is made to show why this must be so ; we are referred to statistics which show that in the past a high correlation of general prices and the total volume of production has been present. If an explanation of this correlation is attempted, it is generally simply to the effect that the expectation of selling at higher prices than present costs will induce everybody to expand production, while in the opposite case the fear of being compelled to sell below costs will prove a strong deterrent. That is to say, it is only the general or average movement of prices which counts.

Now this idea that changes of relative prices and changes in the volume of production are consequent upon changes in the price level, and that money affects individual prices only by means of its influence on the general price level, seems to me to be at the root of at least three very erroneous opinions: *Firstly*, that money acts upon prices and production only if the general price level changes, and, therefore, that prices and production are always unaffected by money,—that they are at their " natural " level,—if the price level remains stable. *Secondly*, that a rising price level tends always to cause an increase of production, and a falling price level always a decrease of production ; and *thirdly*, that " monetary theory might even be described as nothing more than the theory of how the value of money is determined ".[1] It is such delusions, as we shall see, which make it possible to assume that we can neglect the influence of money so long as the value of money is assumed to be stable, and apply without further qualification the reasonings of a general economic theory which pays attention to " real causes " only, and that we have only to add to this theory a separate theory of the value of money and of the consequences of its changes in order to get a complete explanation of the modern economic process.

Further details are unnecessary. You are all sufficiently familiar with this type of theory to supply

[1] R. G. Hawtrey, l.c., p. 64.

these for yourselves and to correct any exaggerations which I may have committed in my endeavour to make the contrast with the other types of theory as strong as possible. Any further strengthening of the contrast can best be ·carried out by my proceeding forthwith to the second of the major stages in the development of monetary theory. I wish only to emphasise, before I pass on to that, that henceforward when I speak of stages of development, I do not mean that each of these stages has in turn taken the place of the foregoing as the recognised doctrine. Quite on the contrary, each of these stages is still represented among contemporary monetary theorists and indeed in all probability the first has still the greatest number of adherents.

(4) As might be expected, the second stage arises by way of dissatisfaction with the first. This dissatisfaction makes its appearance quite early. Locke and Montanari, at the end of the seventeenth century, had stated quite clearly the theory I have been discussing. Richard Cantillon, whose criticism of Locke I have taken as the motto of this lecture, realised its inadequacy, and in his famous *Essai sur le Commerce* (published 1755), he provides the first attempt known to me to trace the actual chain of cause and effect between the amount of money and prices. In a brilliant chapter, which W. S. Jevons called " one of the most marvellous things in the book ", he attempts to show " by what path and in what proportion the increase of money raises the price of things ". Starting from the assumption

of the discovery of new gold or silver mines, he proceeds to show how this additional supply of the precious metals first increases the incomes of all persons connected with their production, how the increase of the expenditure of these persons next increases the prices of things which they buy in increased quantities, how the rise in the prices of these goods increases the incomes of the sellers of these goods, how they, in their turn, increase their expenditure, and so on. He concludes that only those persons are benefited by the increase of money whose incomes rise early, while to persons whose incomes rise later the increase of the quantity of money is harmful.

Better known is the somewhat shorter exposition of the same idea which David Hume gave a little later in a famous passage of his *Political Discourses*,[1] which so closely resembles the words of Cantillon that it is hard to believe that he had not seen one of those manuscripts of the *Essai* which are known to have been in private circulation at the time when the *Discourses* were written. Hume, however, makes it clear that, in his opinion, " it is only in this interval or intermediate situation, between the acquisition of money and the rise of prices, that the increasing quantity of gold and silver is favourable to industry ".

To the Classics, this line of reasoning did not seem susceptible of improvement. While Hume is often

---

[1] Published 1752, republished as part of his *Essays Moral, Political and Literary* (Pt. II, Essay IV, Of Money) which originally appeared in 1742, and therefore are often wrongly quoted with that date.

quoted, his method of approach was not amplified for more than a century. It was not until the increase of the supply of gold consequent upon the Californian and Australian discoveries that there was any new impetus to this type of analysis. J. E. Cairnes' *Essay on the Australian Gold Discoveries*[1] contains probably the most noteworthy refinement of the argument of Cantillon and Hume before it was finally incorporated into more modern explanations based upon the subjective theories of value.

It was inevitable that modern theory should be sympathetic towards a point of view which traces the effects of an increase of money to its influence on individual decisions. But a generation passed before serious attempts were made to base the explanation of the value of money and the effects of changes in the amount of money upon the fundamental concepts of marginal utility theory. I shall not dwell here at any length on the variety of forms this assumes in the different modern theories which base the explanation of the value of money on the subjective elements determining the demand for money on the part of the individual. In the form this theory has received at the hands of Professor

[1] Essays towards a Solution of the Gold Question, in *Essays in Political Economy, Theoretical and Applied*, London, 1873, particularly Essay II : " The Course of Depreciation." These *Essays* were originally published in 1855-60 in *Frazers Magazine* and the *Edinburgh Review*. It may be of interest to mention here that Carl Menger who has decisively influenced modern development in this field, was well acquainted with Cairnes' exposition. *Cf.* on this point my Introduction to Vol. I of the *Collected Works of Carl Menger* in the Series of Reprints of Scarce Tracts in Economics, edited by the London School of Economics.

Mises, it belongs already to the third and fourth of our main stages of development, and I shall have occasion to refer to it later. It is worth noticing, however, that, in so far as these theories are confined to an explanation of the manner in which the effects of increase in the amount of money are distributed through the various channels of trade, they still suffer from a not unimportant defect. While they succeed in providing a general scheme for the deduction of the successive effects of an increase or decrease of the amount of money, provided that we know where the additional money enters into circulation, they do not help us to make any *general* statements about the effects which any change in the amount of money must have. For, as I shall show later, everything depends on the point where the additional money is injected into circulation (or where money is withdrawn from circulation), and the effects may be quite opposite according as the additional money comes first into the hands of traders and manufacturers or directly into the hands of salaried people employed by the State.

(5) Very early, and, in the beginning, with only little relation to the problem of the value of money, there had, however, sprung up a doctrine, or rather a number of closely related doctrines, the importance of which was not appreciated at the time, although in the end they were to be combined to fill the gap I have been discussing. I refer to the doctrines of the influence of the quantity of money on the rate of interest, and

through it on the relative demand for consumers' goods on the one hand and producers' or capital goods on the other. These form the third stage in the development of monetary theory. These doctrines have had to surmount unusual obstacles and prejudices, and until recently they received very little attention. It almost seems as if economists had for so long a time struggled against the popular confusions between the value of money proper and the price for a money loan that in the end they had become almost incapable of seeing that there was any relation at all between the rate of interest and the value of money. It is therefore worth while attempting to trace their development in rather greater detail.

While the existence of some relation between the quantity of money and the rate of interest was clearly recognised very early—traces of an understanding could certainly be found in the writings of Locke and Dutot—the first author known to me to enunciate a clear doctrine on this point was Henry Thornton. In his *Paper Credit of Great Britain*, published in 1802 at the beginning of the discussion on Bank Restriction—a really remarkable performance, the true importance of which is only now beginning to be recognised—he struck for the first time one of the leading notes of the new doctrine. The occasion for his statement was an inquiry into the question whether there existed a natural tendency to keep the circulation of the Bank of England within the limits which would prevent a dangerous depreciation. Thornton denied that such a natural tendency existed and held that, on the contrary, the circulation might expand beyond all assignable limits if the Bank would only keep its rate of interest low enough. He based his opinion on considerations so weighty that I cannot resist quoting them at some length :

" In order to ascertain how far the desire of obtaining loans at the Bank may be expected at any time to be carried, we must enquire into the subject of the quantum of profit likely to be derived from borrowing there under the existing circumstances. This is to be judged of by considering two points : the amount, first, of interest to be paid on the sum borrowed ; and, secondly, of the mercantile or other gain to be obtained by the employment of the borrowed capital. The gain which can be acquired by the means of commerce is commonly the highest which can be had ; and it also regulates, in a great measure, the rate in all other cases. We may, therefore, consider this question as turning principally on a comparison of the rate of interest taken at the bank with the current rate of mercantile profit "[1] (p. 287).

Thornton restated these doctrines in the first of his two speeches on the Bullion Report, which were also published as a booklet[2] and would deserve being recovered from oblivion. In this speech he attempts to call the attention of the House to the subject of the rate of interest as " a very great and turning point ", and, after restating his theory in a shorter form, adds

[1] In order to appreciate the importance of this statement, another passage occurring a little earlier in the same chapter (p. 261) should be consulted. In the course of this passage, Thornton writes : " As soon, however, as the circulating medium *ceases to increase*, the extra profit is at an end." (Italics mine.)

[2] Substance of two speeches by Henry Thornton, Esq., in the debate in the House of Commons on the report of the Bullion Committee on the 7th and 14th May, 1811, London, 1811. *Cf.* particularly p. 19 *et seq.*

a new and different theory on the relations between prices and interest (which must on no account be confused with his other theory) namely a theory of the influence of an expectation of a rise of prices on the money rate of interest, a theory which later on was to be re-discovered by A. Marshall and Irving Fisher. This theory, however, does not concern us here.[1]

Thornton's theory seems to have been generally accepted among the " bullionists ", though it appears to have been forgotten by the time that the doctrine of this school became the target of those attacks of the Banking School to which it would have been a sufficient answer. Within the next two years it had been restated by Lord King[2] and J. L. Foster,[3] and, what is much more important, it was accepted by David Ricardo, in his pamphlet of 1809, who gave it a still more modern ring by speaking of the rate of interest falling below its *natural level* in the interval between the issues of the Bank and their effects on prices.[4] He repeated this also in his *Principles*,[5] which should have been sufficient to make it generally known. The doctrine

[1] *Cf.* T. E. Gregory, Introduction to Tooke and Newmarch's *History of Prices and of the State of the Circulation*, p. 23. Professor Gregory does not, however, clearly distinguish between the two theories.

[2] *Thoughts on the Effects of the Bank Restriction*, London, 1803, p. 20.

[3] *An Essay on the Principles of Commercial Exchanges*, 1804, p. 113.

[4] *The high price of bullion a proof of the depreciation of Bank Notes*. Third edit., 1810, p. 47. *Essays*, ed. E. K. C. Gonner, p. 35.

[5] *Principles of Political Economy and Taxation*, Works, ed. McCulloch, p. 220.

makes its appearance in the Bullion Report,[1] and it remained familiar to economists for some time after the restriction period.

In 1823, Thomas Joplin, the inventor of the currency doctrine, enunciates the same principle which a few years later he elaborated into a peculiar but very interesting theory of the " pressure and anti-pressure of capital upon currency " and propounds it as a new discovery.[2] Though his theory is interwoven with some quite erroneous opinions, which probably prevented his contemporaries from recognising the real contributions contained in his writings, yet, nevertheless, he succeeds in providing the clearest explanation of the relations between the rate of interest and the fluctuations of the note circulation which had been given up to that time. The principle which, in Joplin's opinion, neither Thornton nor those who adopted his opinions discovered, and which probably was responsible for " every great fluctuation in prices that has occurred since the first establishment of our banking system ", is that when the supply of capital exceeds the demand, it has the effect of

[1] *Bullion Report*, etc., octavo edit., 1810, p. 56 ; ed. Cannan, p. 51.

[2] In a work entitled *Outlines of a system of Political Economy ; written with a view to prove to Government and the Country that the cause of the present agricultural distress is entirly artificial, and to suggest a plan for the management of currency by which it may be remedied now and any recurrence of similar evils be prevented in the future*, London, 1823, pp. 62 and 198 *et seq.* This work probably contains also the first exposition of the programme later advocated and put into practice by the members of the " Currency School " Joplin's second work referred to in the Text is *An Analysis and History of the Currency Question*, London, 1832.

compressing the country circulation : when the demand is greater than the supply, it has the effect of expanding it again.[1] He devotes some pages to an exposition of how the rate of interest operates to equalise the demand for and the supply of capital, and how any change of that rate affects productive activity, and then proceeds : " But, with our currency, or rather the currency of the country banks . . . the effects are different.   The interest of money, when it is abundant, is not reduced, but the circulation . . . is diminished ; and on the contrary, when money is scarce, an enlargement of issues takes place, instead of a rise in the rate of interest.   The Country Bankers never vary the interest they charge. . . .   He must, of necessity, have one fixed charge, whatever it may be : for he never can know what the true rate is.   With a metallic currency, on the contrary, the Banker would always know the state of the market.   In the first place, he could not lend money until it had been saved and placed in his hands, and he would have a particular amount to lend.   On the other hand, he would have more or fewer persons wanting to borrow, and in proportion as the demand would exceed or fall short of the amount he had to lend, he would raise or lower his terms : . . .   But, in consequence of the Country Banks being not only dealers in incipient capital, but issuers of currency, the demand for currency and the demand for capital are so mingled

[1] *Analysis and History*, p. 101.

together that all knowledge of either is totally con-
founded."[1]

For the next seventy-five years there was hardly
any progress in this connection. Three years after
Joplin, in 1826, Thomas Tooke (who eighteen years later
was to enlarge upon the erroneousness of what he then
could already call the commonly received doctrine that
a low rate of interest is calculated to raise prices and
a high rate to depress them)[2] accepted Thornton's
doctrine, and developed it in some minor points.[3] In
1832 J. Horsley Palmer reproduced it before the parliamentary committee on the Renewal of the Bank
Charter,[4] and as late as 1840 the doctrine that the
" demand for loans and discounts at a rate below the
usual rate is insatiable " was treated almost as a matter
of course by N. W. Senior,[5] and it even entered, though
in a somewhat emasculated form, into J. S. Mills' *Principles of Political Economy*.[6]

[1] *Analysis and History*, pp. 108-9. *Cf.* also pp. 111-13.

[2] T. Tooke, *An Inquiry into the Currency Principle*, London,
1844, p. 77.

[3] Tooke, *Considerations on the State of the Currency*, London,
1826, p. 22, footnote. As late as 1840 he still reprinted this note
in the appendix to the first volume of his *History of Prices* though
not without omitting some important sentences. *Cf.* Gregory,
Introduction, p. 25.

[4] *Report on the Committee of Secrecy on the Bank of England Charter*,
London, 1833, p. 18. Q. 191-7.

[5] In an anonymous article entitled " Lord King " in the *Edinburgh
Review*, October, 1846, later reprinted in N. W. Senior's *Biographical
Sketches*, London, 1863. The relevant parts of this article are now
al   reproduced in N. W. Senior's *Industrial Efficiency and Social
Economy*, ed. by S. Leon Levy. New York, 1928. Vol. II, pp. 117-18.

[6] Book III, Chap. XXIII, para. 4, ed. Ashley, p. 646 *et seq*.

(6) Before following the more modern development of this theory, I must, however, trace the origins of the second strand of thought which in the end became interwoven with the one just considered to constitute modern doctrine in this matter. While the line of thought we have already considered pays attention only to the relation between the rate of interest, the amount of money in circulation and, as a necessary consequence of the latter, the general price level, the second pays attention to the influence which an increase in the amount of money exercises upon the production of capital, either directly or through the rate of interest. The theory that an increase of money brings about an increase of capital, which has recently become very popular under the name of " forced saving ", is even older than the one we have just been considering.

The first author clearly to state this doctrine and the one who elaborated it in greater detail than any of his successors up to very recent times was J. Bentham. In a passage of his *Manual of Political Economy* written in 1804 but not published until 1843, he deals in some detail with the phenomenon which he calls " Forced Frugality". By this he means the increased " addition to the mass of future wealth " which a government can bring about by applying funds raised by taxation or the creation of paper money to the production of capital goods. But interesting and important as this discussion by Bentham is, and although it is more than probable that it was known to some of the economists of this circle, the fact that it appeared in print only so many years later reduces its importance for the development of the doctrine very much.[1]

The honour of first having discussed the problem in some detail in print is apparently due to T. R. Malthus, who, in 1811, in an unsigned review[2] of Ricardo's first pamphlet, introduces his remarks with the complaint that no writer he is acquainted with " has ever seemed sufficiently aware of the influence which a different distribution of the circulating medium of the country must have on those accumulations which are destined to facilitate future production ". He then demonstrates on an assumed " strong case " that a change of the proportion between capital and revenue to the advantage of capital so " as to throw the produce of the country chiefly in the hands of the productive classes" would have the effect that " in a short time, the produce of the country would be greatly augmented ". The next paragraph must be quoted in full.   He writes :

" Whenever, in the actual state of things, a fresh issue of notes comes into the hands of those who mean to employ them in the prosecution and extension of profitable business, a difference in the distribution of the circulating medium takes place, similar in kind to that which has been last supposed ; and produces similar, though of course comparatively inconsiderable effects, in altering the proportion between capital

[1] Bentham's contribution to this problem is discussed in somewhat greater detail in a note by the present author on " The development of the doctrine of Forced Saving " (*Quarterly Journal of Economics*, November, 1932) where also an even earlier reference to the problem by H. Thornton and a number of later contributions to the discussion on it are mentioned, which are omitted in the present sketch.

[2] *Edinburgh Review*, Vol. XVII.   No. XXXIV, February, 1811, p. 363 *et seq*.   *Cf.* also the reply of Ricardo in appendix to the fourth edition of his pamphlet on the *High Price of Bullion*.

and revenue in favour of the former. The new notes go into the market as so much additional capital, to purchase what is necessary for the conduct of the concern. But, before the produce of the country has been increased, it is impossible for one person to have more of it, without diminishing the shares of some others. This diminution is affected by the rise of prices, occasioned by the competition of the new notes, which puts it out of the power of those who are only buyers, and not sellers, to purchase as much of the annual produce as before : While all the industrious classes,—all those who sell as well as buy,—are, during the progressive rise of prices, making unusual profits ; and, even when this progression stops, are left with the command of a greater portion of the annual produce than they possessed previous to the new issues."

The recognition of this tendency of an increased issue of notes to increase the national capital does not blind Malthus to the dangers and manifest injustice connected with it. He simply offers it, he says, as a rational explanation of the fact that a rise of prices is generally found conjoined with public prosperity.

With a single exception this suggestion of Malthus does not seem to have been appreciated at the time— though the mere fact that Ricardo replied to it at length should have made it familiar to economists. The exception is a series of memoranda on the Bullion Report which Dugald Stewart prepared in 1811 for Lord Lauderdale and which were later reprinted as an appendix to his lectures on Political Economy.[1] Objecting to the oversimplified version of the quantity theory

[1] *Cf.* the Collected Works of Dugald Stewart, edited by Sir William Hamilton, London, 1855, vol. VIII, pp. 440-9. A fuller discussion of D. Stewart's views on the subject will be found in the note on "The Development of the Doctrine of Forced Saving ", quoted before.

employed in the reasoning of the Bullion Report he attempts to explain the more " indirect connection between the high prices and an increased circulating medium ". In the course of this discussion he comes very near to the argument employed by Malthus and in one of the later memoranda actually refers to the article which in the meantime had come to his notice, and reproduces the paragraph quoted above.

There are further allusions to the problem by other authors of the early nineteenth century, notably by T. Joplin and R. Torrens, and John Stuart Mill in the fourth of his *Essays on Some Unsettled Questions of Political Economy*—" On profits and Interest "— (written in 1829 or 1830) goes at least so far as to mention that, as the result of the activity of bankers, " revenue " may be " converted into capital ; and thus, strange as it may appear, the depreciation of the currency, when effected in this way, operates to a certain extent as a forced accumulation."[1]

But he believed then that this phenomenon belonged to the " further anomalies of the rate of interest which have not, so far as we are aware, been hitherto brought within the pale of exact science ". The first edition of his *Principles* seems to contain nothing on this point. But in 1865, in the sixth edition, he added to his chapter on " Credit as a Substitute for Money " a footnote which so closely resembles the statement by Malthus that it seems very probable that something—perhaps

[1] *Essays on Some Unsettled Questions of Political Economy*, London, 1844, p. 118.

the publications of D. Stewart's Collected Works—had directed his attention to the earlier discussion of the point.[1]

(7) In the period after the publication of J. S. Mill's *Principles* for a long time attention was paid only to the first of the two related ideas we have been analysing. For many years there was very little progress at all. Occasional restatements of the views of the earlier authors occurred, but added nothing and received little attention.[2] The doctrine of the " indirect chain of effects connecting money and prices ", as developed by Sidgwick, Giffen, Nicholson, and even Marshall,[3] adds hardly anything to what had been evolved from Thornton to Tooke. More significant is the further development and perhaps independent re-discovery of the forced saving doctrine by Leon Walras in 1879.[4] Although his contribution had been practically forgotten and has only recently been recovered from oblivion by Professor Marget, it is of special interest because it is probably through Walras that this doctrine reached Knut Wicksell. And it was only this great Swedish economist who at the end of the century finally succeeded in definitely welding the two, up to then, separate

[1] J. S. Mill. *Principles of Political Economy*, ed. Ashley, p. 512.
[2] An instance of such restatement of earlier doctrine which is somewhat surprising in view of the later opinions of this author, occurs in Adolf Wagner's early *Beiträge zur Lehre von den Banken*, Leipzig, 1857, pp. 236-9.
[3] *Cf.* J. W. Angell, *The Theory of International Prices*, Cambridge, 1926, p. 117 *et seq.*
[4] Leon Walras, *Theorie Mathématique du Billet de Banque*, 1879, reprinted in *Études d'Économie Politique Appliqué*, Lausanne and Paris, 1898.

strands of thoughts into one. His success in this regard is explained by the fact that his attempt was based on a modern and highly developed theory of interest, that of Böhm-Bawerk. But by a curious irony of fate, Wicksell[1] has become famous, not for his real improvements on the old doctrine, but for the one point in his exposition in which he definitely erred : namely, for his attempt to establish a rigid connection between the rate of interest and the changes in the general price level.

Put concisely, Wicksell's theory is as follows : If it were not for monetary disturbances, the rate of interest would be determined so as to equalise the demand for and the supply of savings. This equilibrium rate, as I prefer to call it, he christens the natural[2] rate of interest. In a money economy, the actual or money rate of interest (" Geldzins ") may differ from the equilibrium or natural rate, because the demand for and the supply of capital do not meet in their natural form but in the form of money, the quantity of which available for capital purposes may be arbitrarily changed by the banks.

[1] Wicksell's first and most important exposition of this doctrine is in his *Geldzins und Güterpreise* (published in German   Jena, 1898) which should be consulted together with Wicksell's later restatement in the second volume of his *Vorlesungen über Nationalökonomie*, Jena, 1922.

[2] Sometimes also the " normal " (p. 111) or " real " rate of interest. This latter form of expression has given rise to a confusion with a different theory concerning the influence of an expectation of price changes on the rate, which is commonly associated with the name of Fisher, but which, as mentioned before, was already known to Thornton, Ricardo and Marshall.

Now, so long as the money rate of interest coincides with the equilibrium rate, the rate of interest remains " neutral " in its effects on the prices of goods, tending neither to raise nor to lower them. When the banks, however, lower the money rate of interest below the equilibrium rate, which they can do by lending more than has been entrusted to them, i.e., by adding to the circulation, this must tend to raise prices ; if they raise the money rate above the equilibrium rate—a case of less practical importance—they exert a depressing influence on prices. From this correct statement, however, which does not imply that the price level would remain unchanged if the money rate corresponds to the equilibrium rate, but only that, in such conditions, there are no *monetary* causes tending to produce a change in the price level, Wicksell jumps to the conclusion that, so long as the two rates agree, the price level must always remain steady. There will be more to say about this later. For the moment, it is worth observing a further development of the theory. The rise of the price level which is supposed to be the necessary effect of the money rate remaining below the equilibrium rate, is in the first instance brought about by the entrepreneurs spending on production the increased amount of money loaned by the banks. This process, as Malthus had already shown, involves what Wicksell now called enforced or compulsory saving.[1]

---

[1] *Geldzins und Güterpreise*, pp. 102, 143.

That is all I need to say here in explanation of the Wicksellian theory. Nor shall I here discuss the important development of this theory added by the Austrian economist, Professor Mises.[1] An exposition of the present form of this theory will form the main subject of my next two lectures. Here it is only necessary to point out that Professor Mises has improved the Wicksellian theory by an analysis of the different influences which a money rate of interest different from the equilibrium rate exercises on the prices of consumers' goods on the one hand, and the prices of producers' goods on the other. In this way, he has succeeded in transforming the Wicksellian theory

[1] *Theorie des Geldes und der Umlaufsmittel*, 1912. Simultaneously with Professor Mises a distinguished Italian economist, Professor Marco Fanno, made in an exceedingly interesting and now very rare book on *Le Banche e il Mercato Monetario*, an independent attempt to develop Wicksell's theory further. A revised shorter German version of the views of this author is now available in his contribution to the *Beiträge zur Geldtheorie*, Vienna, 1933.

Considerable elements of Professor Mises' theory and particularly the doctrine of " Forced Saving " seem to have been introduced into America through Professor Schumpeter's *Theorie der Wirtschaftlichen Entwicklung* and Dr. B. M. Anderson's *Value of Money* and gained considerable vogue since. In any case since the publication of this book in 1917 " Forced Saving " has been discussed by Professors F. W. Taussig (*Principles of Economics*, 3rd edit., pp. 351, 359), F. Knight (*Risk, Uncertainty and Profit*, p. 166 note and Index), D. Friday (*Profit, Wages and Prices*, pp. 216-17), and A. H. Hansen (*Cycles of Prosperity and Depression*, 1921, pp. 104-6). Whether the American author whose views on these problems comes nearest to those expressed in the present book, Mr. M. W. Watkins, whose exceedingly interesting article on " Commercial Banking and the Formation of Capital " (*Journal of Political Economy*, vol. xxvii., 1919), I have only recently become acquainted with, is indebted to the same source I do not know.

In England similar ideas seem to have been developed independently, first by Professor Pigou (in *Is Unemployment Inevitable ?* 1925, pp. 100-11) and then in much greater detail by Mr. D. H. Robertson (*Banking Policy and the Price Level*, 1926, *passim*).

into an explanation of the credit cycle which is logically satisfactory.

(8) But this brings me to the next part of my discussion. For it is partly upon the foundations laid by Wicksell and partly upon criticism of his doctrine that what seems to me the fourth of the great stages of the progress of monetary theory is being built. (I ought, perhaps, expressly to warn you that while up to this point of our survey I have been describing developments which have already taken place, what I am about to say about the fourth stage concerns rather what I think it should be than what has already taken definite shape.)

It would take too much time to trace chronologically the steps by which, by degrees, the Wicksellian theory has been transformed into something new. You will be better able to appreciate this change if I turn immediately to the discussion of those deficiencies of his doctrine which eventually made it necessary definitely to break away from certain of the fundamental concepts in the theory which had been taken over by him from his predecessors.

I have mentioned already that, according to Wicksell the equilibrium rate of interest was a rate which simultaneously restricted the demand for real capital to the amount of savings available *and* secured stability of the price level. His idea was obviously one which is very generally held even at the present time, namely, that as, at an equilibrium rate of interest, money would remain neutral towards prices, therefore in such circumstances there could be no reason at all for a change of the price level.

Nevertheless, it is perfectly clear that, in order that the supply and demand for real capital should be equalised, the banks must not lend more or less than has been deposited with them as savings (and such additional amounts as may have been saved and hoarded). And this means naturally that (always excepting the case just mentioned) they must never allow the effective amount of money in circulation to change.[1] At the same time, it is no less clear that, in order that the price level may remain unchanged, the amount of money in circulation must change as the volume of production increases or decreases. The banks could *either* keep the demand for real capital within the limits set by the supply of savings, *or* keep the price level steady ; but they cannot perform both functions at once. Save in a society in which there were no additions to the supply of savings, i.e., a stationary society, to keep the money rate of interest at the level of the equilibrium rate would mean that in times of expansion of production the price level would fall. To keep the general price level steady would mean, in similar circumstances, that the loan rate of interest would have to be lowered below the equilibrium rate.

[1] From now onward the term " amount of money in circulation " or even shortly " the quantity of money " will be used for what should more exactly be described as the effective money stream or the amount of money payments made during a unit period of time. The problems arising out of possible divergences between these two magnitudes will only be taken up in Lecture IV.

The consequences would be what they always are when the rate of investment exceeds the rate of saving.

It would be possible to cite other cases where the influence of money on prices and production is quite independent of the effects on the general price level. But it seems obvious as soon as one once begins to think about it that almost any change in the amount of money, whether it does influence the price level or not, must *always* influence relative prices. And, as there can be no doubt that it is relative prices which determine the amount and the direction of production, almost any change in the amount of money must necessarily also influence production.

But if we have to recognise that, on the one hand, under a stable price level, relative prices may be changed by monetary influences, and, on the other that relative prices may remain undisturbed only when the price level changes, we have to give up the generally received opinion that if the general price level remains the same, the tendencies towards economic equilibrium are not disturbed by monetary influences, and that disturbing influences from the side of money cannot make themselves felt otherwise than by causing a change of the general price level.

This doctrine, which has been accepted dogmatically by almost all monetary theorists, seems to me to lie at the root of most of the shortcomings of present-day monetary theory and to be a bar to almost all further progress. Its bearing on various proposals for stabilisation is obvious. In these lectures, however, it is in the theoretical foundations of these schemes rather than in the formulation of alternative practical proposals that we are interested. And here, it may be suggested, it is possible very greatly to underestimate the changes in economic theory which are implied if once we drop these unjustified assumptions. For when we investigate into all the influences of money on individual prices, quite irrespective of whether they are or are not accompanied by a change of the price level, it is not long before we begin to realise the superfluity of the concept of a general value of money, conceived as the reverse of some price level. And, indeed, I am of the opinion that, in the near future, monetary theory will not only reject the explanation in terms of a direct relation between money and the price level, but will even throw overboard the concept of a general price level and substitute for it investigations into the causes of the changes of relative prices and their effects on production. Such a theory of money, which will be no longer a theory of the value of money in general, but a theory of the influence of money on the different ratios of exchange between goods of all kinds, seems to me the probable fourth stage in the development of monetary theory.

This view of the probable future of the theory of money becomes less startling if we consider that the concept of relative prices includes the prices of goods of the same kind at different moments, and that here, as in the case of interspatial price relationships, only one relation between the two prices can correspond to a condition of " intertemporal " equilibrium, and that this need not, *a priori*, be a relation of identity or the one which would exist under a stable price level. (This has a particular bearing on the problem of money as a standard of deferred payments, because in this function money is to be conceived simply as the medium which effects an intertemporal exchange.) If this view is correct, the question which in my opinion will take the place of the question whether the value of money has increased or decreased will be the question whether the state of equilibrium of the rates of intertemporal exchange is disturbed by monetary influences in favour of future or in favour of present goods.[1]

(9) It will be the object of the following lectures to show how it is possible to solve at least some of the most important problems of monetary theory without recourse to the concept of a value of money in general. It will then remain for you to make up your mind whether we can conceivably entirely dispense with it. For the moment, I wish only to remind you of one further reason why it seems that, in the case of money, in contrast to any other good, the question of its value in general is of no consequence.

We are interested in the prices of individual goods because these prices show us how far the demand for any particular good can be satisfied. To discover the causes why certain needs, and the needs of certain

[1] I have dealt more fully with the difficult question of the conditions of intertemporal equilibrium of exchange in an article " Das intertemporale Gleichgewichtsystem der Preise und die Bewegungen des ' Geldwertes ' " in the *Weltwirtschaftliches Archiv.*, vol. 28, 1928.

persons, can be satisfied to a greater degree than others is the ultimate object of economics. There is, however, no *need* for money in this sense,—the absolute amount of money in existence is of no consequence to the well-being of mankind—and there is, therefore, no objective value of money in the sense in which we speak of the objective value of goods. *What we are interested in is only how the relative values of goods as sources of income or as means of satisfaction of wants are affected by money.*

The problem is never to explain any " general value " of money but only how and when money influences the relative values of goods and under what conditions it leaves these relative values undisturbed, or, to use a happy phrase of Wicksell, when money remains *neutral* relatively to goods.[1] Not a money which is *stable* in value but a *neutral* money must therefore form the starting point for the theoretical analysis of monetary influences on production, and the first object of monetary theory should be to clear up the conditions under which money might be considered to be neutral in this sense. We stand as yet at the very beginning of this kind of investigation. And, though I hope that what I say in the next lectures may help a little, I am fully conscious that all results we obtain at this stage should only be regarded as tentative. So far as I am concerned, it is the method of approach more than the details of the results which is of importance in what follows.

[1] *Cf.* the Appendix to Lecture IV.

Lecture II

THE CONDITIONS OF EQUILIBRIUM BETWEEN THE PRODUCTION OF CONSUMERS' GOODS AND THE PRODUCTION OF PRODUCERS' GOODS

" The question of how far, and in what manner, an increase of currency tends to increase capital appears to us so very important, as fully to warrant our attempt to explain it. . . . It is not the *quantity* of the circulating medium which produces the effects here described, but the *different distribution* of it . . . on every fresh issue of notes . . . a larger proportion falls into the hands of those who consume and produce, and a smaller proportion into the hands of those who only consume."

T. R. Malthus,
Edinburgh Review, vol. XVII (1811),
p. 363 *et seq.*

(1) Before we can attempt to understand the influence of prices on the amount of goods produced, we must know the nature of the immediate causes of a variation of industrial output. Simple as this question may at first appear, contemporary theory offers at least three explanations.

(2) First of these, we may take the view that the main causes of variations of industrial output are to be found in changes of the willingness of individuals to expand effort. I mention this first, because it is probably the theory which has at present the greatest

number of adherents in this country. That this point of view is so widely accepted in England is probably due to the fact that a comparatively great number of economists here are still under the influence of "real cost" theories of value which make this type of explanation of any change in the total value of output the natural one. Mr. D. H. Robertson's stimulating book on *Banking Policy and the Price Level* provides, perhaps, the best example of reasoning based on this assumption. Yet I do not think that this assumption is at all justified by our common experience ; it is a highly artificial assumption to which I would only be willing to resort when all other explanations had failed. But its correctness is a question of fact, and I shall make no attempt to refute it directly. I shall only try to show that there are other ways of accounting for changes in industrial output which seem less artificial.

(3) The second type of explanation is the one which " explains " variations of production simply by the changes of the amount of factors of production used. In my opinion this is no explanation at all. It depends essentially upon a specious appeal to facts. Starting from the existence of unused resources of all kinds, known to us in daily experience, it regards any increase of output simply as the consequence of bringing more unused factors into use, and any diminution of output as the consequence of more resources becoming idle. Now, that any such change in the amount of resources employed implies a corresponding change in output is, of course, beyond question. But

it is not true that the existence of unused resources is a *necessary* condition for an increase of output, nor are we entitled to take such a situation as a starting point for theoretical analysis. If we want to explain fluctuations of production, we have to give a complete explanation. Of course this does not mean that we have to start for that purpose *ab ovo* with an explanation of the whole economic process. But it does mean that we have to start where general economic theory stops ; that is to say at a condition of equilibrium when no unused resources exist. The existence of such unused resources is itself a fact which needs· explanation. It is not explained by static analysis and, accordingly, we are not entitled to take it for granted. For this reason I cannot agree that Professor Wesley Mitchell is justified when he states that he considers it no part of his task " to determine how the fact of cyclical oscillations in economic activity can be reconciled with the general theory of equilibrium, or how that theory can be reconciled with facts ".[1] On the contrary, it is my conviction that if we want to explain economic phenomena at all, we have no means available but to build on the foundations given by the concept of a tendency towards an equilibrium. For it is this concept alone which permits us to explain fundamental phenomena like the determination of prices or incomes, an understanding of which is essential to any explanation of fluctuation of production. If

[1] *Business Cycles, The Problem and its Setting*, New York, 1927, p. 462.

we are to proceed systematically, therefore, we must start with a situation which is already sufficiently explained by the general body of economic theory. And the only situation which satisfies this criterion is the situation in which all available resources are employed. The existence of unused resources must be one of the main objects of our explanation.[1]

(4) To start from the assumption of equilibrium has a further advantage. For in this way we are compelled to pay more attention to causes of changes in the industrial output whose importance might otherwise be underestimated. I refer to changes in the methods of using the existing resources. Changes in the direction given to the existing productive forces are not only the main cause of fluctuations of the output of individual industries ; the output of industry as a whole may also be increased or decreased to an enormous extent by changes in the use made of existing resources. Here we have the third of the contemporary explanations of fluctuations which I referred to at the beginning of the lecture. What I have here in mind are *not* changes in the methods of production made possible by the progress of technical knowledge, but the increase of output made possible by a transition to more capitalistic methods of production, or, what is the same thing, by organising production so that, at any given moment, the available resources

---

[1] I have dealt more fully with the relation between pure economic theory and the explanation of business fluctuations in my book, *Monetary Theory and the Trade Cycle* (London, 1933), Chaps. I and II.

are employed for the satisfaction of the needs of a future more distant than before. It is to this effect of a transition to more or less " roundabout " methods of production that I wish particularly to direct your attention. For, in my opinion, it is only by an analysis of this phenomenon that in the end we can show how a situation can be created in which it is temporarily impossible to employ all available resources.

The processes involved in any such transition from a less to a more capitalistic form of production are of such a complicated nature that it is only possible to visualise them clearly if we start from highly simplified assumptions and work through gradually to a situation more like reality. For the purpose of these lectures, I shall divide this investigation into two parts. Today I shall confine myself to a consideration of the conditions under which an equilibrium between the production of producers' goods and the production of consumers' goods is established, and the relation of this equilibrium to the flow of money ; I reserve for the next lecture a more detailed explanation of the working of the price mechanism during the period of transition, and of the relations between changes in the price system and the rate of interest.

(5) My first task is to define the precise meaning of certain terms. The term production I shall always use in its widest possible sense, that is to say, all processes necessary to bring goods into the hands of the consumer. When I mean land and labour, I shall speak of *original means of production*. When I

use the phrase *factors of production* without further qualification this will cover capital also, that is to say this term will include all factors from which we derive *income* in the form of wages, rent, and interest. When I use the expression *producers' goods*, I shall be designating all goods existing at any moment which are not consumers' goods, that is to say, *all* goods which are directly or indirectly used in the production of consumers' goods, *including* therefore the original means of production, as well as instrumental goods and all kinds of unfinished goods. Producers' goods which are not original means of production, but which come between the original means of production and consumers' goods, I shall call *intermediate products*. None of these distinctions coincides with the customary distinction between durable and non-durable goods, which I do not need for my present purpose. I shall, however, have to use this distinction and to add a new one, which stands in some relation to it, in my next lecture.

(6) I have already pointed out that it is an essential feature of our modern, " capitalistic ", system of production that at any moment a far larger proportion of the available original means of production is employed to provide consumers' goods for some more or less distant future than is used for the satisfaction of immediate needs. The *raison d'être* of this way of organising production is, of course, that by lengthening the production process we are able to obtain a greater quantity of consumers' goods out of

a given quantity of original means of production. It is not necessary for my present purpose to enter at any length into an explanation of this increase of productivity by roundabout methods of production. It is enough to state that within practical limits we may increase the output of consumers' goods from a given quantity of original means of production indefinitely, provided we are willing to wait long enough for the product. The thing which is of main interest for us is that any such change from a method of production of any given duration to a method which takes more or less time implies quite definite changes in the organisation of production, or, as I shall call this particular aspect of organisation, to distinguish it from other more familiar aspects, changes in the *structure of production*.

In order to get a clear view of what is actually implied by these changes in the structure of production it is useful to employ a schematic representation.[1] For this purpose, I find it convenient to represent the successive applications of the original means of production which are needed to bring forth the output of consumers' goods accruing at any moment of time,

---

[1] The following diagrams were originally the result of an attempt to replace the somewhat clumsy tables of figures, used for the same purpose in my Paradox of Saving (*Economica*, May, 1931), by a more easily grasped form of representation. Later I noticed that similar triangular figures had been used as representations of the capitalistic process of production not only by W. S. Jevons (*Theory of Political Economy*, 4th edit., 1911, pp. 230-7), but particularly also by K. Wicksell (*Lectures on Political Economy*, vol. I, p. 152 *et seq.*) and, following him, G. Åckerman (*Realkapital und Kapitalzins*, Part I. Stockholm, 1923). Dr. Marschak has recently made the very appropriate suggestion to designate these triangular figures as the " Jevonian Investment Figures".

by the hypotenuse of a right-angled triangle, such as the triangle in Fig. I. The value of these original

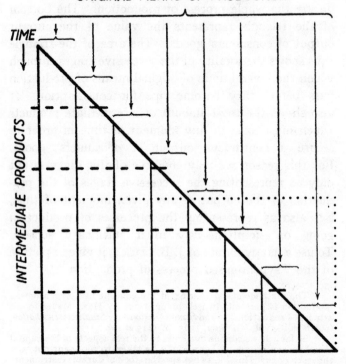

ORIGINAL MEANS OF PRODUCTION

TIME

INTERMEDIATE PRODUCTS

OUTPUT OF CONSUMERS GOODS
FIG. I.

means of production is expressed by the horizontal projection of the hypotenuse, while the vertical dimension, measured in arbitrary periods from the top to the bottom, expresses the progress of time, so that the inclination of the line representing the amount of original means of production used means that these original means of production are expended continuously during the whole process of production. The bottom of the triangle represents the value of the current output of consumers' goods. The area of the triangle thus shows the totality of the successive stages through which the several units of original means of production pass before they become ripe for consumption. It also shows the total amount of intermediate products which must exist at any moment of time in order to secure a continuous output of consumers' goods. For this reason we may conceive of this diagram not only as representing the successive stages of the production of the output of any given moment of time, but also as representing the processes of production going on simultaneously in a stationary society. To use a happy phrase of J. B. Clark's, it gives a picture of the " synchronised process of production ".[1,2]

[1] The methodological bearing of the concept of a synchronised production is particularly well brought out by Hans Mayer in his article," Produktion", in the *Handwörterbuch der Staatswissenschaften*, fourth edit., vol. VI, Jena, 1925, p. 1115 *et seq.*

[2] So long as we confine ourselves to the real aspects of the capital structure the triangular figures may be taken to represent not only the stock of goods in process but also the stock of durable instruments existing at any moment of time. The different instalments of future services which such goods are expected to render will in that case have to be imagined to belong to different " stages " of production corresponding to the time interval which will elapse before these services mature. (For a more detailed discussion of the problems arising out of the two different aspects, of actual duration of production and the durability of goods, in which time enters in the productive process, *cf.* my article " On the Relationship between Investment and Output ", *Economic Journal*, June, 1934.) But as

Now it should be clear without further explanation that the proportion between the amount of intermediate products (represented by the area of the triangle) which is necessary at any moment of time to secure a continuous output of a given quantity of consumers' goods, and the amount of that output,[1] must grow with

---

soon as it is tried to use the diagrammatic representations to show the successive transfers of the intermediate products from stage to stage in exchange for money it becomes evidently impossible to treat durable goods in the same way as goods in process since it is impossible to assume that the individual services embodied in any durable goods will regularly change hands as they approach a stage nearer to the moment when they will actually be consumed. For this reason it has been necessary, as has been pointed out in the preface, to abstract from the existence of durable goods so long as the assumption is made that the total stock of intermediate products as it gradually proceeds towards the end of the process of production is exchanged against money at regular intervals.

[1] It would be more exact to compare the stock of intermediate products existing *at a moment* of time not with the output of consumers' goods *during a period* of time, but rather with the rate at which consumers' goods mature at the same moment of time. Since, however, this output at a moment of time would be infinitely small, that proportion could only be expressed as a differential quotient of a function which represents the flow of intermediate products at the point where this flow ends, i.e., where the intermediate products become consumers' goods. This relationship is essentially the same as that between the total quantity of water in a stream and the rate at which this water passes the mouth of this stream. (This *simile* seems to be more appropriate than the more familiar one which considers capital as a " stock " and only income as a " flow ". *Cf.* on this point N. J. Polak, *Grundzüge der Finanzierung*, Berlin, 1926, p. 13.) It is convenient to treat the quantity of intermediate products at any point of this stream as a function of time $f(t)$ and accordingly the total quantity of intermediate products in the stream, as an integral of this function over a period r equal to the total length of the process of production. If we apply this to any process of production beginning at the moment x, the total quantity of intermediate products in the stream will be expressed by $\int_{x}^{x+r} f(t).\, dt$, and the output of consumers' goods at a moment of time by $f(x+r)$. In the diagrams used in the text the function $f(t)$ is represented by the hypotenuse, its concrete

the length of the roundabout process of production. As the average time interval between the application of the original means of production and the completion of the consumers' goods increases, production becomes more capitalistic, and *vice versa*. In the case we are contemplating in which the original means of production are applied at a constant rate throughout the whole process of production, this average time is exactly half as long as the time which elapses between the application of the first unit of original means of production and the completion of the process. Accordingly, the total amount of intermediate products may also be represented by a rectangle half as high as the triangle, as indicated by the dotted line in the diagram. The areas of the two figures are necessarily equal, and it sometimes assists the eye to have a rectangle instead of a triangle when we have to judge the relative magnitude represented by the area of the figure. Furthermore, it should be noticed that, as the figure represents values and not physical production, the surplus return obtained by the roundabout methods of production is not represented in the diagram. In this lecture I have intentionally neglected interest. We shall have to take that into consideration next time. Until then we may assume that the intermediate products remain

value $f(x + r)$ by the horizontal side and the integral by the area of the triangle. There is of course no reason to assume that the function $f(t)$ will be linear, i.e., that the amount of original factors applied during successive stages of the process is constant, as is assumed in the diagrams. On these and some connected points see the article on "Investment and Output", quoted in the preceding footnote.

the property of the owners of the original means of production until they have matured into consumers' goods and are sold to consumers. Interest is then received by the owners of the original means of production together with wages and rent.

(7) A perfectly continuous process of this sort is somewhat unwieldy for theoretical purposes : moreover such an assumption is not perhaps sufficiently realistic. It would be open to us to deal with the difficulties by the aid of higher mathematics. But I, personally, prefer to make it amenable to a simpler method by dividing the continuous process into distinct periods, and by substituting for the concept of a continuous flow the assumption that goods move intermittently in equal intervals from one stage of production to the next. In this way, in my view, the loss in precision is more than compensated by the gain in lucidity.

Probably the simplest method of transforming the picture of the continuous process into a picture of what happens in a given period is to make cross sections through our first figure at intervals corresponding to the periods chosen, and to imagine observers being posted at each of these cross cuts who watch and note down the amount of goods flowing by. If we put these cross sections, as indicated by the broken lines in Fig. 1, at the end of each period, and represent the amount of goods passing these lines of division in a period by a rectangle of corresponding size, we get the new illustration of the same process given in Fig. 2.

It is convenient for the purposes of exposition to count only that part of the total process of production

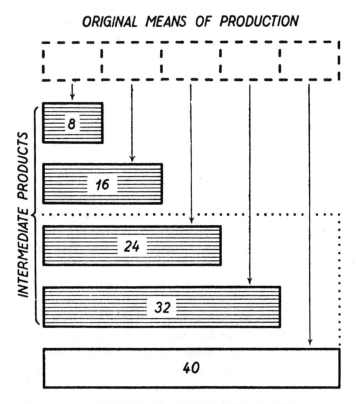

ORIGINAL MEANS OF PRODUCTION

INTERMEDIATE PRODUCTS

8

16

24

32

40

OUTPUT OF CONSUMERS GOODS

Fig. 2.

which is completed during one of these periods, as a separate stage of production. Each of the successive

shaded blocks in the diagram will then represent the
product of the corresponding stage of production as it is
passed on to the next while the differences in the length
of the successive blocks correspond to the amount of
original means of production used in the succeeding
stage. The white block at the bottom represents
the output of consumers' goods during the period. In
a stationary state, which is still the only state I am
considering, this output of consumers' goods is necessarily equal to the total income from the factors of
production used, and is exchanged for this income.
The proportion of the white area to the shaded area,
in this diagram 40:80 or 1:2, expresses the proportion
between the output of consumers' goods and the output
of intermediate products (or between the amount of
consumption and the amount of new and renewed
investment during any period of time).

So far, I have used this schematic illustration of
the process of production only to represent the movements of goods. It is just as legitimate to use it as an
illustration of the movement of money. While goods
move downwards from the top to the bottom of our
diagram, we have to conceive of money moving in the
opposite direction, being paid first for consumers' goods
and thence moving upwards until, after a varying
number of intermediary movements, it is paid out as
income to the owners of the factors of production,
who in turn use it to buy consumers' goods. But in
order to trace the relation between actual money payments, or the proportional quantities of money used

in the different stages of production, and the movements of goods, we need a definite assumption in regard to the division of the total process among different firms, which alone makes an exchange of goods against money necessary. For this does not by any means necessarily coincide with our division into separate stages of production of equal length. I shall begin with the simplest assumption, that these two divisions do coincide, that is to say that goods moving towards consumption do change hands against money in equal intervals which correspond to our unit production periods.

In such a case, the proportion of money spent for consumers' goods and money spent for intermediate products is equal to the proportion between the total demand for consumers' goods and the total demand for the intermediate products necessary for their continuous production ; and this, in turn, must correspond, in a state of equilibrium, to the proportion between the output of consumers' goods during a period of time and the output of intermediate products of all earlier stages during the same period. Given the assumptions we are making, all these proportions are accordingly equally expressed by the proportion between the area of the white rectangle and the total shaded area. It will be noticed that the same device of the dotted line as was used in the earlier figure is employed to facilitate the comparison of the two areas. The dotted rectangle shows that, in the kind of production represented by Fig. 2, which actually takes four successive stages, the average length of the roundabout process is only two stages, and the amount of intermediate products is therefore twice as great as the output of customers' goods.

(8) Now if we adopt this method of approach, certain fundamental facts at once become clear. The first fact which emerges is that the amount of money spent on producers' goods during any period of time may be far greater than the amount spent for consumers' goods during the same period. It has been computed, indeed, that in the United States, payments for consumers' goods amount only to about one-twelfth of the payments made for producers' goods of all kinds.[1] Nevertheless, this fact has not only very often been overlooked, it was even expressly denied by no less an authority than Adam Smith. According to Smith[2] : " The value of goods circulated between the different dealers never can exceed the value of those circulated between dealers and consumers ; whatever is bought by the dealer being ultimately destined to be sold to the consumers." This proposition clearly rests upon a mistaken inference from the fact that the total expenditure made in production must be covered by the return from the sale of the ultimate products ; but it remained unrefuted, and

[1] Cf. M. W. Holtrop, De Omloopssnelheid van het Geld, Amsterdam, 1928, p. 181.
[2] Wealth of Nations, Book II, Chap. I, ed. Cannan, p. 305. It is interesting to note that this statement of Adam Smith is referred to by Thomas Tooke as a justification of the erroneous doctrines of the Banking School. (Cf. An Inquiry into the Currency Principle, London, 1844, p. 71.)

quite recently in our own day it has formed the foundation of some very erroneous doctrines.[1] · The solution of the difficulty is, of course, that most goods are exchanged several times against money before they are sold to the consumer, and on the average exactly as many times as often as the total amount spent for producers' goods is larger than the amount spent for consumers' goods.

Another point which is of great importance for what follows, and which, while often overlooked in current discussion,[2] is quite obvious if we look at our diagram, is the fact that what is generally called the capital equipment of society—the total of intermediate products in our diagram—is not a magnitude which, once it is brought into existence, will necessarily last for ever independently of human decisions. Quite the contrary : whether the structure of production remains the same depends entirely upon whether entrepreneurs find it profitable to re-invest the usual

[1] *Cf.* W. T. Foster and W. Catchings, *Profits*, Publications of the Pollak Foundation for Economic Research, No. 8, Boston and New York, 1925, and a number of other books by the same authors and published in the same series. For a detailed criticism of their doctrines, *cf.* my article, " The ' Paradox ' of Saving," *Economica*, May, 1931.

[2] J. S. Mill's emphasis on the " perpetual consumption and reproduction of capital ", like most of his other penetrating, but often somewhat obscurely expressed observations on capital, has not had the deserved effect, although it directs attention to the essential quality of capital which distinguishes it from other factors of its production. More recently the misplaced emphasis which some authors, particularly Professors J. B. Clark, J. Schumpeter and F. H. Knight, have put on the tautological statement that so long as stationary conditions prevail capital is *ex definitione* permanent, has further contributed to obscure the problem.

proportion of the return from the sale of the product of their respective stages of production in turning out intermediate goods of the same sort. Whether this is profitable, again, depends upon the prices obtained for the product of this particular stage of production on the one hand and on the prices paid for the original means of production and for the intermediate products taken from the preceding stage of production on the other. The continuance of the existing degree of capitalistic organisation depends, accordingly, on the prices paid and obtained for the product of each stage of production and these prices are, therefore, a very real and important factor in determining the direction of production.

The same fundamental fact may be described in a slightly different way. The money stream which the entrepreneur representing any stage of production receives at any given moment is always composed of net income which he may use for consumption without disturbing the existing method of production, and of parts which he must continuously re-invest. But it depends entirely upon him whether he re-distributes his total money receipts in the same proportions as before. And the main factor influencing his decisions will be the magnitude of the profits he hopes to derive from the production of his particular intermediate product.

(9) And now at last we are ready to commence to discuss the main problem of this lecture, the problem of how a transition from less to more capitalistic methods of production, or *vice versa*, is actually brought about,

and what conditions must be fulfilled in order that a new equilibrium may be reached. The first question can be answered immediately : a transition to more (or less) capitalistic methods of production will take place if the total demand for producers' goods (expressed in money) increases (or decreases) relatively to the demand for consumers' goods. This may come about in one of two ways : either as a result of changes in the volume of voluntary saving (or its opposite), or as a result of a change in the quantity of money which alters the funds at the disposal of the entrepreneurs for the purchase of producers' goods. Let us first consider the case of changes in voluntary saving, that is, simple shifts of demand between consumers' goods and producers' goods.[1]

As a starting point, we may take the situation depicted in Fig. 2, and suppose that consumers save and invest an amount of money equivalent to one fourth of their income of one period. We may assume further that these savings are made continuously, exactly as they can be used for building up the new process of production. The proportion of the demand for consumers' goods to the demand for intermediate products will then ultimately be changed from 40 : 80

[1] I am deliberately discussing here the " strong case " where saving implies a reduction in the demand for *all* consumers' goods, although this is a highly unlikely case to occur in practice, since it is in this case that many people find it so difficult to understand how a general decrease in the demand for consumers' goods should lead to an increase of investment. Where, as will regularly be the case, the reduction in the demand for consumers' goods affect only a few kinds of such goods, these special difficulties would, of course, be absent.

to 30:90, or 1:2 to 1:3. The additional amounts of money available for the purchase of intermediate products must now be so applied that the output of consumers' goods may be sold for the reduced sum of thirty now available for that purpose. It should now be sufficiently clear that this will only be the case if the average length of the roundabout processes of production and, therefore, in our instance, also the number of successive stages of production, is increased in the same proportion as the demand for intermediate products has increased relatively to the demand for consumers' goods, i.e., from an average of two to an average of three (or from an actual number of four to an actual number of six) stages of production. When the transition is completed, the structure of production will have changed from that shown in Fig. 2 to the one shown in Fig. 3. (It should be remembered that the relative magnitudes in the two figures are values expressed in money and not physical quantities, that the amount of original means of production used has remained the same, and that the amount of money in circulation and its velocity of circulation are also supposed to remain unchanged.)

If we compare the two diagrams, we see at once that the nature of the change consists in a stretching of the money stream flowing from the consumers' goods to the original means of production. It has, so to speak, become longer and narrower. Its breadth at the bottom stage, which measures the amount of money spent during a period of time on consumers' goods and,

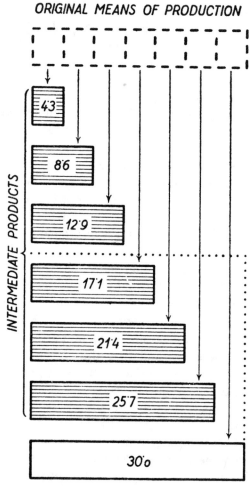

ORIGINAL MEANS OF PRODUCTION

INTERMEDIATE PRODUCTS

4·3

8·6

12·9

17·1

21·4

25·7

30·0

OUTPUT OF CONSUMERS GOODS

Fig. 3.

at the same time, the amount of money received as income in payment for the use of the factors of production, has permanently decreased from forty to thirty. This means that the price of a unit of the factors of production, the total amount of which (if we neglect the increase of capital) has remained the same, will fall in the same proportion, and the price of a unit of consumers' goods, the output of which has increased as a consequence of the more capitalistic methods of production, will fall in still greater proportion. The amount of money spent in each of the later stages of production has also decreased, while the amount used in the earlier stages has increased, and the total spent on intermediate products has increased also because of the addition of a new stage of production.[1]

Now it should be clear that to this change in the distribution of the amounts of money spent in the different stages of production there will correspond a similar change in the distribution of the total amount of goods existing at any moment. It should also be clear that the effect thus realised,—given the assumptions we are making,—is one which fulfils the object of saving and investing, and is identical with the effect which would have been produced if the savings were made in kind instead of in money. Whether it has been

[1] To avoid misunderstandings I have now substituted the terms "earlier" and "later" stages used by Professor Taussig in this connection, for the expression "higher" and "lower" which are unequivocal only with reference to the diagrams but are liable to be confused with such expressions as "highly finished" products, particularly as A. Marshall has used the terms in this reverse sense (cf. *Industry and Trade*, p. 219).

brought about in the most expeditious way, and whether the price changes which follow from our assumptions provide a suitable stimulus to the re-adjustment are not questions with which we need concern ourselves at this juncture. Our present purpose is fulfilled if we have established, that under the assumptions we have made, the initial variation in the proportional demand for consumers' goods and for intermediate products respectively becomes permanent, that a new equilibrium may establish itself on this basis, and that the fact that the amount of money remains unchanged, in spite of the increase of the output of consumers' goods and of the still greater increase of the total turnover of goods of all kinds and stages, offers no fundamental difficulties to such an increase of production, since total expenditure on the factors of production, or total costs, will still be covered by the sums received out of the sales of consumers' goods.

But now the question arises : does this remain true if we drop the assumptions that the amount of money remains unchanged and that, during the process of production, the intermediate products are exchanged against money at equal intervals of time ?

(10) Let us begin by investigating the effects of a change in the amount of money in circulation. It will be sufficient if we investigate only the case most frequently to be encountered in practice : the case of an increase of money in the form of credits granted to producers. Again we shall find it convenient to start from the situation depicted in Fig. 2 and to suppose

that the same change in the proportion between the demand for consumers' goods and the demand for intermediate products, which, in the earlier instance, was supposed to be produced by voluntary saving, is now caused by the granting of additional credits to producers. For this purpose, the producers must receive an amount of forty in additional money. As will be seen from Fig. 4, the changes in the structure of production which will be necessary in order to find employment for the additional means which have become available will exactly correspond to the changes brought about by saving. The total services of the original means of production will now be expended in six instead of in four periods ; the total value of intermediate goods produced in the different stages during a period will have grown to three times instead of twice as large as the value of consumers' goods produced during the same period ; and the output of each stage of production, including the final one, measured in physical units will accordingly be exactly as great as in the case represented in Fig. 3. The only difference at first apparent is that the money values of these goods have grown by one-third compared with the situation depicted in Fig. 3.

There is, however, another and far more important difference which will become apparent only with the lapse of time. When a change in the structure of production was brought about by saving, we were justified in assuming that the changed distribution of demand between consumers' goods and producers' goods

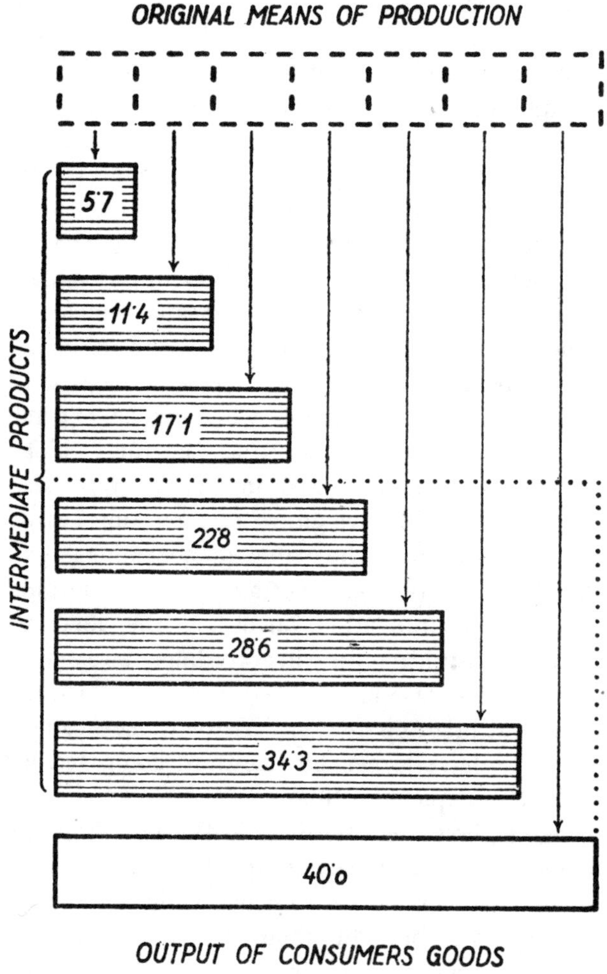

ORIGINAL MEANS OF PRODUCTION

INTERMEDIATE PRODUCTS

5.7

11.4

17.1

22.8

28.6

34.3

40.0

OUTPUT OF CONSUMERS GOODS

FIG. 4.

would remain permanent, since it was the effect of voluntary decisions on the part of individuals. Only because a number of individuals had decided to spend a smaller share of their total money receipts on consumption and a larger share on production was there any change in the structure of production. And since, after the change had been completed, these persons would get a greater proportion of the increased total real income, they would have no reason again to increase the *proportion* of their money receipts spent for consumption.[1] There would accordingly exist no inherent cause for a return to the old proportions.

In the same way, in the case we are now considering, the use of a larger proportion of the original means of production for the manufacture of intermediate products can only be brought about by a retrenchment of consumption. But now this sacrifice is not voluntary, and is not made by those who will reap the benefit from the new investments. It is made by consumers in general who, because of the increased competition from the entrepreneurs who have received the additional money, are forced to forego part of what they used to consume. It comes about not because they want to consume less, but because they get less goods for their money income. There can be no doubt that, if their money receipts should rise again, they would immediately attempt to expand consumption to the usual proportion. We shall see in the next lecture why,

[1] It is important to bear in mind that, though the total money income would diminish, the total real income would increase.

in time, their receipts will rise as a consequence of the increase of money in circulation. For the moment let us assume that this happens. But if it does, then at once the money stream will be re-distributed between consumptive and productive uses according to the wishes of the individual concerned, and the artificial distribution, due to the injection of the new money, will, partly at any rate, be reversed. If we assume that the old proportions are adhered to, then the structure of production too will have to return to the old proportion, as shown in Fig. 5. That is to say production will become less capitalistic, and that part of the new capital which was sunk in equipment adapted only to the more capitalistic processes will be lost. We shall see in the next lecture that such a transition to less capitalistic methods of production necessarily takes the form of an economic crisis.

But it is not necessary that the proportion between the demand for consumers' goods and the demand for intermediate products should return exactly to its former dimensions as soon as the injection of new money ceases. In so far as the entrepreneurs have already succeeded, with the help of the additional money, in completing the new processes of longer duration,[1] they will, perhaps, receive increased money

[1] It should, however, be remembered that a process cannot be regarded as completed in this sense, just because an entrepreneur at any one stage of production has succeeded in completing his section of it. A complete process, in the sense in which this concept is used in the text, comprises *all* the stages of any one line of production, whether they are part of one firm or divided between several. I have further elaborated this point in my article on " Capital and Industrial Fluctuations ", *Econometrica*, April, 1934.

returns for their output which will put them in a position to continue the new processes, i.e., to expend permanently a larger share of their money receipts upon

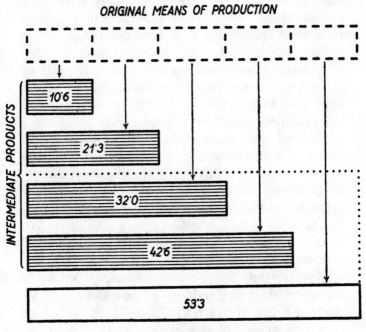

ORIGINAL MEANS OF PRODUCTION

10·6

21·3

32·0

42·6

INTERMEDIATE PRODUCTS

53·3

OUTPUT OF CONSUMERS GOODS

Fig. 5.

intermediate products without reducing their own consumption. It is only in consequence of the price changes caused by the increased demand for consumers' goods that, as we shall see, these processes too become unprofitable.

But for the producers who work on a process where the transition to longer roundabout processes is not yet completed when the amount of money ceases to increase the situation is different. They have spent the additional money which put them in a position to increase their demand for producers' goods and in consequence it has become consumers' income ; they will, therefore, no longer be able to claim a larger share of the available producers' goods, and they will accordingly have to abandon the attempt to change over to more capitalistic methods of production.

(11) All this becomes easier to follow if we consider the simpler case in which an increase in demand for consumers' goods of this sort is brought about directly by additional money given to consumers. In recent years, in the United States, Messrs. Foster and Catchings have urged that, in order to make possible the sale of an increased amount of consumers' goods produced with the help of new savings, consumers must receive a proportionately larger money income. What would happen if their proposals were carried out ? If we start with the situation which would establish itself as a consequence of new savings if the amount of money remained unchanged (as shown in Fig. 3), and then assume that consumers receive an additional amount of money sufficient to compensate for the relative increase of the demand for intermediate products caused by the savings (i.e., an amount of 15) and spend it on consumers' goods, we get a situation in which the proportion between the demand for consumers' goods, and

the demand for producers' goods, which, in consequence of the new savings, had changed from 40:80 to 30:90 or from 1:2 to 1:3 would again be reduced to 45:90

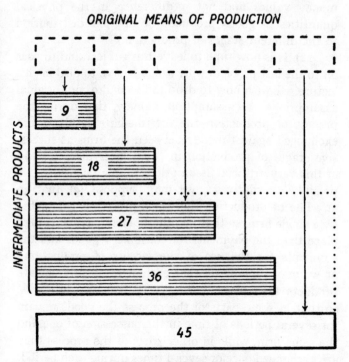

ORIGINAL MEANS OF PRODUCTION

9

18

27

36

INTERMEDIATE PRODUCTS

45

OUTPUT OF CONSUMERS GOODS

Fig. 6.

or 1:2. That this would mean a return to the less capitalistic structure of production which existed before the new savings were made, and that the only effect of such an increase of consumers' money incomes would be to frustrate the effect of saving follows clearly from Fig. 6. (The difference from the original situation depicted in Fig. 2 is again only a difference in money values and not a difference in the physical quantities of goods produced or in their distribution to the different stages of production.)

(12) It is now time to leave this subject and to pass on to the last problem with which I have to deal in this lecture. I wish now to drop the second of my original assumptions, the assumption, namely, that during the process of production the intermediate products are exchanged against money between the firms at successive stages of production in equal intervals. Instead of this very artificial assumption, we may consider two possible alternatives: we may suppose (a) that in any line of production the whole process is completed by a single firm, so that no other money payments take place than the payments for consumers' goods and the payments for the use of the factors of production: or we may suppose (b) that exchanges of intermediate products take place, but at very irregular intervals, so that in some parts of the process the goods remain for several periods of time in the possession of one and the same firm, while in other parts of the process they are exchanged once or several times during each period.

(13) (a) Let us consider first the case in which the whole process of production in any line of production is completed by a single firm. Once again we may use Fig. 1 to illustrate what happens. In this case the base of the triangle represents the total payments for consumers' goods and the hypotenuse (or, more correctly,

its horizontal projection) represents the amounts of money paid for the original means of production used. No other payments would be made and any amount of money received from the sale of consumers' goods could immediately be spent for original means of production. It is of fundamental importance to remember that we can assume only that any *single* line of production is in this way integrated into one big firm. It would be entirely inappropriate in this connection to suppose that the production of *all* goods is concentrated in one enterprise. For, if this were the case, of course the manager of this firm could, like the economic dictator of a communistic society, arbitrarily decide what part of the available means of production should be applied to the production of consumers' goods and what part to the production of producers' goods. There would exist for him no reason to borrow and, for individuals, no opportunity to invest savings. Only if *different* firms compete for the available means of production will saving and investing in the ordinary sense of the word take place, and it is therefore such a situation which we must make the starting point of our investigation.

Now, if any of these integrated industries decides to save and invest part of its profits in order to introduce more capitalistic methods of production, it must not immediately pay out the sums saved for original means of production. As the transition to more capitalistic methods of production means that it will be longer until the consumers' goods produced by the new process are ready, the firm will need the sums saved to pay wages, etc., during the interval of time between the sale of the last goods produced by the old process, and the getting ready of the first goods produced by the new process. So that, during the whole period of transition, it must pay out less to consumers than it receives in order to be able to bridge the gap at the end of this period, when it has nothing to sell but has to continue to pay wages and rent. Only when the new product comes on the market and there is no need for further saving will it again currently pay out all its receipts.

In this case, therefore, the demand for consumers' goods, as expressed in money, will be only temporarily reduced, while in the case where the process of production was divided between a number of independent stages of equal length, the reduction of the amount available for the purchase of consumers' goods was a permanent one. In the present case, the prices of the consumers' goods will, accordingly, fall only in inverse proportions as their quantity has increased, while the total paid as income for the use of the factors of production will remain the same. These conclusions are, however, only provisional as they do not take account of the relative position of the one firm considered to all other firms which will certainly be affected by a change of relative prices and interest rates which are necessarily connected with such a process. Unfortunately, these influences are too complicated to allow of treatment within the scope of these lectures, and I must ask you, therefore, to suspend judgment upon the ultimate effects of the price changes which will take place under these conditions.

But there is one point to which I must particularly direct your attention : The reason in this case why the unchanged amount of money used in production remains sufficient, in spite of the fact that a larger amount of intermediate products now exists, whereas in the former case, the use of an increased amount of intermediate products required the use of an increased quantity of money is this. In the former case the intermediate products passed from one stage of production to the next by an exchange against money. But in the present case this exchange is replaced by internal barter, which makes money unnecessary. Of course, our division of the continuous process of production into separate stages of equal length is entirely arbitrary : it would be just as natural to divide it into stages of different lengths and then speak of these stages as exhibiting so many more or less instances of internal barter. But the procedure which has been adopted serves to bring out a concept, which I shall need in a later lecture, the concept of the relative volume of the flow of goods during any period of time, as compared with the amount of goods exchanged against money in the same period. If we divide the path traversed by the elements of any good from the first expenditure of original means of production until it gets in the hands of the final consumer into unit periods, and then measure the quantities of goods which pass each of these lines of division during a period of time, we secure a comparatively simple measure of the flow of goods without having recourse to higher mathematics. Thus, we may say that, in the instance we have been considering, money has become more efficient in moving goods, in the sense that a given amount of exchanges against money has now become sufficient to make possible the movement of a greater volume[1] of goods than before.

(14) (b) Perhaps this somewhat difficult concept becomes more intelligible if I illustrate it by supposing that two of the independent firms which we have supposed to represent the successive stages of production in our diagrams 2 and 6 are combined into one firm. This is the second of the alternative possibilities I set out to consider. Once this has happened, the passage of the intermediate products from the one to the next stage of production will take place without money payments being necessary, and the flow of goods from the moment they enter the earlier of the two stages until they leave the later will be effected by so much less money. A corresponding amount of money will thus be released and may be used for other purposes. The reverse effect will, of course, be witnessed

[1] Even if this total of goods moving towards consumption during each period is not actually exchanged against money in each period, it is not an imaginary, but a real and important magnitude, since the value of this total is a magnitude which continually rests within our power to determine. It probably stands in close relation to what is commonly called free capital, and it is certainly the supply of this factor which—together with new saving—determines the rate of interest ; the capital which remains invested in durable instruments affects the interest rate from the demand side only, i.e., by influencing opportunities for new investment.

if the two firms separate again. An increased amount of money payments will be required to effect the same movement of goods and the proportion of money payments to the flow of goods advancing towards consumption will have increased.

(15) Unfortunately, all names which might be used to designate this kind of monetary effectiveness have already been appropriated for designating different concepts of the velocity of money. Until somebody finds a fitting term, therefore, we shall have to speak somewhat clumsily of the proportion between the amount of goods exchanged against money and the total flow of goods or of the proportion of the total movements of goods which is effected by exchange against money.

Now this proportion must on no account be confused with the proportion of the volume of money payments to the physical volume of trade. The proportion I have in mind may remain the same while the volume of trade increases relatively to the total of money payments and the price level falls, if only the same proportion of the total flow of goods is exchanged against money, and it may change though the proportion of the total of money payments to the physical volume of trade remains the same. It is, therefore, not necessarily influenced either by changes in the amount of money or by changes in the physical volume of trade ; it depends only upon whether, in certain phases of the process of production, goods do or do not change hands.

So far I have illustrated this concept only by instances from the sphere of production. It may be applied also to the sphere of consumption. Here, too, sometimes a larger and sometimes a smaller share of the total output of consumers' goods is exchanged for money before it is consumed. Accordingly, here, too, we may speak about the proportion which the total output of consumers' goods in a period of time bears to the output which is sold for money. And this proportion may be different in the different stages of production. But in its effect upon the structure of production, the efficiency of a given amount of money spent in any stage of production (including the last stage—consumption) is determined by the proportion in that stage ; and any change in that proportion has the same effects as an alteration in the amount of money spent in this particular stage of production.

So much for the complications which arise when we drop the assumption that production is carried on in independent stages of equal length. It has been necessary to discuss them here at some length in order to clear the way for an investigation, into which I wish to enter in the last lecture, in connection with the arguments for and against an elastic money supply. But for the tasks which I shall have to face tomorrow, it will be expedient again to make use of the simplest assumption and to suppose that production is carried on in independent stages of equal length, as we did in our schematic representations, and that this proportion is not only the same in all stages of production, but also that it remains constant over time.

THE WORKING OF THE PRICE MECHANISM IN THE COURSE OF THE CREDIT CYCLE

" The first effect of the increase of productive activity, initiated by the policy of the banks to lend below the natural rate of interest is . . . to raise the prices of producers' goods while the prices of consumers' goods rise only moderately . . . But soon a reverse movement sets in : prices of consumers' goods rise and prices of producers' goods fall, i.e., the loan rate rises and approaches again the natural rate of interest."

L. v. Mises,
Theorie des Geldes und der Umlaufsmittel, 1912, p. 431.

(1) In the last lecture I dealt with the problems of changes in the structure of production consequent upon any transition to more or less capitalistic methods of production, in terms of the total sums of money available for the purchase of the product of each stage of production. It might seem, therefore, that now I come to the problem of explaining those changes in relative prices which bring it about that goods are directed to new uses—the central problem of these lectures[1]—the explanation should run in terms of sectional price levels, that is to say in terms of changes

[1] As has already been mentioned in the first chapter, the effects of a divergence between the money-rate and the equilibrium-rate of interest on relative prices were originally shortly discussed by Professor Mises. On the actual working of the price mechanism

in the price levels of the goods of the different stages of production. But to do this would mean that at this stage of the explanation I should fall back upon just that method of using price averages which I condemned at the outset.

At the same time, it should by now be clear that, at this stage of the explanation, a treatment in terms of price averages would not be adequate to our purposes. What we have to explain is why certain goods which have thus far been used in one stage of production can now be more profitably used in another stage of production. Now this will only be the case if there are changes in the proportions in which the different producers' goods may be profitably used in any stage of production, and this in turn implies that there must be changes in the prices offered for them in different stages of production.

---

which brings about the changes in the structure of production his work contains however hardly more than the sentences quoted at the beginning of this lecture. It seems that most people have found them difficult to understand and that they have remained completely unintelligible to all who were not very familiar with Böhm-Bawerk's theory of interest on which they are based. The main difficulty lies in Professor Mises' short statement that the rise of the prices of consumers' goods is the cause of the crisis, while it seems natural to assume that this would rather make production more profitable. This is the main point which I have here tried to clear up. So far the most exhaustive previous exposition of these inter-relationships, which anticipates in some points what is said in the following pages is to be found in R. Strigl, " Die Produktion unter dem Einfluss einer Kreditexpansion", *Schriften des Vereins für Sozialpolitik*, 173/2 München, 1928, particularly p. 203 *et seq.* More recently Professor Strigl has further developed his views on the subject in a book, *Kapital und Produktion*, Vienna, 1934. Some references to earlier anticipations of the ideas developed in this lecture will now be found in an additional note at the end of this lecture.

(2) At this point, it is necessary to introduce the new[1] distinction between producers' goods to which I alluded in the last lecture : the distinction between producers' goods which may be used in all, or at least, many stages of production, and producers' goods which can be used only in one, or at the most, a few stages of production. To the first class belong not only almost all original means of production, but also most raw materials and even a great many implements of a not very specialised kind—knives, hammers, tongs, and so on.[2] To the second class belong most highly special-ised kinds of machinery or complete manufacturing establishments, and also all those kinds of semi-manufactured goods which can be turned into finished goods only by passing a definite number of further stages of production. By adapting a term of von Wieser's, we may call the producers' goods which can be used only in one or a few stages of production,

[1] Since the publication of the first edition of this book my atten-tion has been drawn to the fact that this distinction is clearly implied in some of Böhm-Bawerk's discussions of these problems. *Cf.* his *Positive Theorie des Kapitalzinses* (third edit.), pp. 195 and 199.

[2] This class will, in particular, comprise most of the goods which at one and the same time belong to different stages. " Of course ", says Marshall (*Principles*, first edit., p. 109n.), " a good many belong to several orders at the same time. For instance, a railway train may be carrying people on a pleasure excursion, and so far it is a good of the first order ; if it happens to be carrying at the same time some tins of biscuits, some milling machinery and some machinery that is used for making milling machinery, it is at the same time a good of the second, third and fourth order." In cases like this a transfer of its services from a later to an earlier stage (or, to use Menger's terminology, from a lower to a higher order) is, of course, particularly easy. A plant manufacturing equipment for the produc-tion of consumers' goods as well as for the production of further machinery will sometimes be used mainly for the former and some-times mainly for the latter purpose.

producers' goods of a specific character, or more shortly " specific " goods, to distinguish them from producers' goods of a more general applicability, which we may call " non-specific " goods.[1] Of course, this distinction is not absolute, in the sense that we are always in a position to say whether a certain good is specific or not. But we should be able to say whether any given good is *more or less* specific as compared with another good.

(3) It is clear that producers' goods of the same kind which are used in different stages of production cannot, for any length of time, bring in different returns or obtain different prices in these different stages. On the other hand, it is no less clear that temporary differences between the prices offered in the different stages of production are the only means of bringing about a shift of producers' goods from one stage to another. If such a temporary difference in the relative attractiveness of the different stages of production arises, the goods in question will be shifted from the less to the more attractive stages until, by the operation of the principle of diminishing returns the differences have been wiped out.

Now, if we neglect the possibility of changes in technical knowledge, which may change the usefulness of any particular producers' goods, it is obvious that the immediate cause of a change in the return obtained from producers' goods of a certain kind used in different stages of production must be a change in the price of

[1] *Cf.* Friedrich von Wieser, *Social Economics*, translated by A. Ford Hinrichs, New York, 1927, Book I, Chap. 15.

the product of the stage of production in question.
But what is it which brings about variations of the
relative price of such products ? At first glance it
might seem improbable that the prices of the successive
stages of one and the same line of production should
ever fluctuate relatively to one another because they
are equally dependent upon the price of the final
product. But, having regard to what was said in the
last lecture concerning the possibility of shifts between
the demand for consumers' goods and the demand for
producers' goods, and the consequent changes in the
relation between the amount of original means of production expended and the output of consumers' goods,
and how an elongation of the process of production
increases the return from a given quantity of original
means of production—this point should present no
difficulty.

Now so far I have not expressly referred to the price
margins which arise out of these relative fluctuations
of the prices of the products of successive stages of
production. This has been because I have intentionally neglected interest, or, what amounts to the same
thing, I have treated interest as if it were a payment
for a definitely given factor of production, like wages
or rent. In a state of equilibrium these margins are
entirely absorbed by interest. Hence my assumption
concealed the fact that the total amount of money
received for the product of any stage will regularly
exceed the total paid out for all goods and services
used in this stage of production. Yet that margins

of this kind must exist is obvious from the consideration that, if it were not so, there would exist no inducement to risk money by investing it in production rather than let it remain idle. To investigate the relationship of these margins to the peculiar advantages of the roundabout methods of production would lead us too far into the problems of the general theory of interest. We must therefore be content to accept it as one of the definite conclusions of this theory that —other things remaining the same—these margins must grow smaller as the roundabout processes of production increase in length and *vice versa*. There is one point, however, which we cannot take for granted. The fact that in a state of equilibrium those price margins and the amounts paid as interest coincide does *not* prove that the same will also be true in a period of transition from one state of equilibrium to another. On the contrary, the relation between these two magnitudes must form one of the main objects of our further investigations.

The close interrelation between these two phenomena suggests two different modes of approach to our problem : Either we may start from the changes in the relative magnitude of the demand for consumers' goods and the demand for producers' goods, and examine the effects on the prices of individual goods and the rate of interest ; or we may start from the changes in the rate of interest as an immediate effect of the change in the demand for producers' goods and work up to the changes in the price system which are necessary to establish a new equilibrium between price margins and the rate of interest. It will be found that whichever of these two alternatives we choose as a starting point, our investigation will, in the end, lead us to those aspects of the problem which are the starting point for the other. For the purposes of this lecture, I choose the first as being more in line with my previous argument.

(4) I begin, as I began in the last lecture, with the supposition that consumers decide to save and invest a larger proportion of their income. The immediate effect of the increase in the demand for producers' goods and the decrease in demand for consumers' goods will be that there will be a relative rise in the prices of the former and a relative fall in the prices of the latter. But the prices of producers' goods will not rise equally, nor will they rise without exception. In the stage of production immediately preceding that in which the final touches are given to consumers' goods, the effect of the fall in the prices of consumers' goods will be felt more strongly than the effect of the increase of the funds available for the purchase of producers' goods of all kinds. The price of the product of this stage will, therefore, fall, but it will fall less than the prices of consumers' goods. This means a narrowing of the price margin between the last two stages. But this narrowing of the price margin will make the employment of funds in the last stage less profitable relatively to the earlier stages, and therefore some of the funds which had been used there will tend to be

shifted to the earlier stages. This shift of funds will tend to narrow the price margins in the preceding stages, and the tendency thus set up towards a cumulative rise of the prices of the products of the earlier stages will very soon overcome the tendency towards a fall. In other words, the rise of the price of the product of any stage of production will give an extra advantage to the production of the preceding stage, the products of which will not only rise in price because the demand for producers' goods in general has risen, but also because, by the rise of prices in the preceding stages, profits to be obtained in this stage have become comparatively higher than in the later stages. The final effect will be that, through the fall of prices in the later stages of production and the rise of prices in the earlier stages of production, price margins between the different stages of production will have decreased all round.

This change of relative prices in the different stages of production must inevitably tend to effect the prospects of profits in the different stages, and this, in turn, will tend to cause changes in the use made of the available producers' goods. A greater proportion of those producers' goods which can be used in different stages of production—the non-specific goods—will now be attracted to the earlier stages, where, since the change in the rate of saving, relatively higher prices are to be obtained. And the shifting of goods and services of this type will go on until the diminution of returns in these stages has equalised the profits to be made in all stages. In the end, the returns and the prices obtained for these goods in the different stages of production will be generally higher and a larger proportion of them will be used in the earlier stages of production than before. The general narrowing of the price margins between the stages of production will even make it possible to start production in new and more distant stages which have not been profitable before, and in this way, not only the average time which elapses between the application of the first unit of original mean of production and the completion of the final product, but also the absolute length of the process of production—the number of its stages—will be increased.[1]

But while the effect on the prices of non-specific producers' goods has been a general rise, the effect on the prices of goods of a more specific character—those goods which can only be used in one or a very few stages of production—will be different. If a good of this sort is only adapted to a comparatively late stage of production, the relative deficiency of the non-specific producers' goods required in the same stage of production will lower its return, and if it is itself a product, its production will be curtailed. If,

[1] This lengthening of the structure of production need, however, by no means take exclusively or even mainly the form that the methods used in any individual line of production are changed. The increased prices in the earlier stages of production (the lowered rate of interest) will favour production in the lines using much capital and lead to their expansion at the expense of the lines using less capital. In this way the aggregate length of the investment structure of society might in the extreme case take place without a change of the method employed in any one line of production.

on the other hand, the good belongs to a relatively early stage of production, its price and the amount of it produced will increase. At the same time, the additional stages of production which have been started as a consequence of this transition to more capitalistic methods of production will probably require new goods of a specific character. Some of these will be new products, some natural resources which formerly it was not profitable to use.

Exactly the reverse of all these changes will take place if the demand for consumers' goods increases relatively to the demand for producers' gocds. This will cause not only an increase of the difference between the prices of consumers' goods or products of the last stage of production, and the prices of the products of the previous stage, but also an all round increase of the price margins between the products of the successive stages of production. Prices in the later stages will rise relatively to prices in the earlier stages, producers' goods of a non-specific character will move from the earlier stages to the later, and the goods of specific character in the earlier stages of production will lose part of their value or become entirely useless, while those in the later stages of production will increase in value. I shall discuss certain exceptions to this parallelism later on.

It will, perhaps, facilitate the understanding of these complications if we think of production in its successive stages as a fan, the sticks of which correspond to the prices of the different stages. If more demand is concentrated towards the one extreme—consumers' goods—the fan opens, the differences between the stages become larger, and goods gravitate towards the stages where higher prices are obtained, that is, towards the stages nearer consumption. The most distant stages are abandoned, and within the remaining stages more goods are concentrated toward the one end. The opening of the price fan is thus accompanied by a reduction of the number of stages of production, i.e., of the number of sticks.[1] If, however, a shift of demand from consumers' goods towards producers' goods takes place, the price fan will close, i.e., the differences between the stages will become smaller and goods will tend to gravitate towards the higher stages where prices are now relatively higher, and new and hitherto unused possibilities of further extension of the process of production will be exploited. The closing of the price fan has brought a greater number of stages of production within the range of practical possibilities and thus initiated the transition to longer roundabout methods of production.

(5) A more exact representation of this process can be given by means of a diagram. This has the special advantage of making quite clear a point which is of considerable importance but on which a merely verbal explanation is likely to mislead. It is necessary in such

[1] At this point the simile becomes liable to mislead and it is important to keep in mind all the time that the " fan " refers to price relationships only, but that the length of the structure of production will move in the reverse direction compared with the width of the fan. When the price fan opens, the structure of production is shortened, and *vice versa*.

an exposition, if one wants to avoid too cumbersome expressions, to speak of actual changes in the relative prices of goods in the different stages, where it would be more correct to speak of tendencies towards such a change, or of changes in the demand function for the particular commodity. Whether and to what extent such changes in demand will lead to an actual change in price will of course depend on the elasticity of supply, which in the particular case depends in turn in every stage on the degree of specificity of the intermediate products and the factors from which they are made.

The way in which this shifting of the demand curves for any single factor in the different stages of production operates can be illustrated in the following way. In the diagram below the successive curves represent the marginal productivity of different quantities of one factor in the successive stages of production, the earlier stages being shown on the left and the later stages towards the right. To make the main point come out clearer it has been assumed that the physical quantity of the product due to every additional unit of the factor decreases at the same rate in all stages and that in consequence the general shape of the curves is the same.

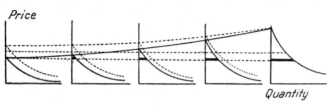

FIG. 7.

The value of the marginal product attributable to every
unit of factors will, however, be equal to the value of
the physical product which is due to it only in the very
last stage where no interval of time elapses between the
investment of the factors and the completion of the
product. If we assume, then, the curve on the right
to represent not only the physical magnitude but also
the value of the marginal product of successive units
of factors applied in that stage, the other curves representing the physical marginal product of the factors
invested in earlier stages will have to be somewhat
adjusted if they are to represent the discounted value of
the marginal product of successive units of factors
applied in the respective stages. And if we assume the
points to which these curves refer, to be equidistant
stages as were those discussed before, the adjustment
necessary at any given rate of interest can be shown
by drawing a discount curve (or a family of discount
curves) connecting every point on the curve on the
right with the corresponding points of the curves further
on the left, and lowering each of these curves by the
amount indicated by the discount curves. (Since every
point on these curves will have to be adjusted separately,
i.e., will have to be lowered not by the same amount
but by the same percentage, this will involve a change
not only of the position but also of the shape of these
curves.) The set of fully drawn curves in the above
diagram shows the position at a given rate of interest
indicated by the one discount curve which is also fully
drawn. And since these curves show the discounted

value of the marginal product of one kind of factor which must of course be the same in the different stages of production, they enable us to determine how much of this factor will be used in every stage if either its price or the total quantity of it to be used in this process are known. This distribution of the factor between the different stages at an arbitrarily assumed price is shown by the fully drawn horizontal lines.

Assume now that the rate of interest is reduced. The new position is indicated by the dotted discount curve and the correspondingly changed shape and position of the marginal productivity curves for the individual stages. Under these conditions the old distribution of factors between the stages would evidently not represent an equilibrium position but one at which the discounted value of the marginal product would be different in every stage. And if the total quantity of the factor which is available remains the same the new equilibrium distribution will apparently be one at which not only the price of the factor will be higher but at which also a considerably greater quantity of it is used in the earlier stages and correspondingly less in the later stages.

This accounts for the change in the price and the distribution of factors which can be used in different stages. To what extent and in what proportion the prices of different factors will be affected by a given change in the rate of interest will depend on the stages in which they can be used and on the shape of their marginal productivity curves in these stages. The price of a factor which can be used in most early stages and whose marginal productivity there falls very slowly will rise more in consequence of a fall in the rate of interest than the price of a factor which can only be used in relatively lower stages of reproduction or whose marginal productivity in the earlier stages falls very rapidly.

It is essentially this difference between the price changes of the different factors which accounts for the changes of the relative prices of the intermediate products at the successive stages. At first it might seem as if, since relative prices of the different intermediate products must correspond to their respective costs, they could change only to the relatively small extent to which the direct interest element in their cost changes. But to think of interest only as a direct cost factor is to overlook its main influence on production. What is much more important is its effect on prices through its effect on demand for the intermediate products and for the factors from which they are produced. It is in consequence of these changes in demand and the changes in cost which it brings about by raising the prices of those factors which are in strong demand in early stages compared to those which are less demanded there, that the prices of the intermediate products are adjusted.

(6) As the initial changes in relative prices which are caused by a change of the relative demand for consumers' goods and producers' goods give rise to a considerable shifting of goods to other stages of production, definite price relationships will only establish

themselves after the movements of goods have been completed. For reasons which I shall consider in a moment, this process may take some time and involve temporary discrepancies between supply and demand. But there is one medium through which the expected ultimate effect on relative prices should make itself felt immediately, and which, accordingly, should serve as a guide for the decisions of the individual entrepreneur : the rate of interest on the loan market. Only in comparatively few cases will the people who have saved money and the people who want to use it in production be identical. In the majority of cases, therefore, the money which is directed to new uses will first have to pass into other hands. The question *who* is going to use the additional funds available for investment in producers' goods will be decided on the loan market. Only at a lower rate of interest than that formerly prevailing will it be possible to lend these funds, and how far the rate of interest will fall will depend upon the amount of the additional funds and the expectation of profits on the part of the entrepreneurs willing to expand their production. If these entrepreneurs entertain correct views about the price changes which are to be expected as a result of the changes in the method of production, the new rate of interest should correspond to the system of price margins which will ultimately be established. In this way, from the outset, the use of the additional funds which have become available will be confined to those entrepreneurs who hope to obtain the highest profits out of their use, and all extensions of production, for which the additional funds would not be sufficient, will be excluded.

(7) The significance of these adjustments of the price mechanism comes out still more clearly when we turn to investigate what happens if the " natural " movement of prices is disturbed by movements in the supply of money, whether by the injection of new money into circulation or by withdrawal of part of the money circulating. We may again take as our two typical cases, (a) the case of additional money used first to buy producers' goods and (b) the case of additional money used first to buy consumers' goods. The corresponding cases of a diminution of the amount of money we may neglect because a diminution of the demand for consumers' goods would have essentially the same effects as a proportional increase of the demand for producers' goods, and *vice versa*.[1] I have already outlined in the last lecture the general tendencies involved in such cases. My present task is to fill in the details of that rough sketch and to show what happens in the interval before a new equilibrium is attained.

As before, I commence with the supposition that the additional money is injected by way of credits to producers. To secure borrowers for this additional amount of money, the rate of interest must be kept

[1] As I have tried to show in another place (*Econometrica*, April, 1934, p. 164) it is even conceivable, although highly unlikely to occur in practice, that hoarding of money income before spent on consumers' goods, might give rise to some additional investment.

sufficiently below the equilibrium rate to make profitable the employment of just this sum and no more. Now the borrowers can only use the borrowed sums for buying producers' goods, and will only be able to obtain such goods (assuming a state of equilibrium in which there are no unused resources) by outbidding the entrepreneurs who used them before. At first sight it might seem improbable that these borrowers who were only put in a position to start longer processes by the lower rate of interest should be able to outbid those entrepreneurs who found the use of those means of production profitable when the rate of interest was still higher. But when it is remembered that the fall in the rate will also change the relative profitableness of the different factors of production for the existing concerns, it will be seen to be quite natural that it should give a relative advantage to those concerns which use proportionately more capital. Such old concerns will now find it profitable to spend a part of what they previously spent on original means of production, on intermediate products produced by earlier stages of production, and in this way they will release some of the original means of production they used before. The rise in the prices of the original means of production is an additional inducement. Of course it might well be that the entrepreneurs in question would be in a better position to buy such goods even at the higher prices, since they have done business when the rate of interest was higher, though it must not be forgotten that they too will have to do business on a smaller margin. But the fact that certain producers' goods have become dearer will make it profitable for them to replace these goods by others. In particular, the changed proportion between the prices of the original means of production and the rate of interest will make it profitable for them to spend part of what they have till now spent on original means of production on intermediate products or capital. They will, e.g., buy parts of their products, which they used to manufacture themselves, from another firm, and can now employ the labour thus dismissed in order to produce these parts on a large scale with the help of new machinery. In other words, those original means of production and non-specific producers' goods which are required in the new stages of production are set free by the transition of the old concerns to more capitalistic methods which is caused by the increase in the prices of these goods. In the old concerns (as we may conveniently, but not quite accurately, call the processes of production which were in operation before the new money was injected) a transition to more capitalistic methods will take place ; but in all probability it will take place without any change in their total resources : they will invest less in original means of production and more in intermediate products.

Now, contrary to what we have found to be the case when similar processes are initiated by the investment of new savings, this application of the original means of production and non-specific intermediate products to longer processes of production will be effected without any preceding reduction of consumption. Indeed, for a time, consumption may even go on at an unchanged rate after the more roundabout processes have actually started, because the goods which have already advanced to the lower stages of production, being of a highly specific character, will continue to come forward for some little time. But this cannot go on. When the reduced output from the stages of production, from which producers' goods have been withdrawn for use in higher stages, has matured into consumers' goods, a scarcity of consumers' goods will make itself felt, and the prices of those goods will rise. Had saving preceded the change to methods of production of longer duration, a reserve of consumers' goods would have been accumulated in the form of increased stocks, which could now be sold at unreduced prices, and would thus serve to bridge the interval of time between the moment when the last products of the old shorter process come on to the market and the moment when the first products of the new longer processes are ready. But as things are, for some time, society as a whole will have to put up with an involuntary reduction of consumption.

But this necessity will be resisted. It is highly improbable that individuals should put up with an unforeseen retrenchment of their real income without making an attempt to overcome it by spending more money on consumption. It comes at the very moment when a great many entrepreneurs know themselves to be in command—at least nominally—of greater resources and expect greater profits. At the same time incomes of wage earners will be rising in consequence of the increased amount of money available for investment by entrepreneurs. There can be little doubt that in the face of rising prices of consumers' goods these increases will be spent on such goods and so contribute to drive up their prices even faster. These decisions will not change the amount of consumers' goods immediately available, though it may change their distribution between individuals. But—and this is the fundamental point—*it will mean a new and reversed change of the proportion between the demand for consumers' goods and the demand for producers' goods in favour of the former*. The prices of consumers' goods will therefore rise relatively to the prices of producers' goods. And this rise of the prices of consumers' goods will be the more marked because it is the consequence not only of an increased demand for consumers' goods but an increase in the demand as measured in money. All this must mean a return to shorter or less roundabout methods of production if the increase in the demand for consumers' goods is not compensated by a further proportional injection of money by new bank loans granted to producers. And at first this is probable. The rise of the prices of consumers' goods will offer prospects of temporary extra profits to entrepreneurs. They will be the more ready to borrow at the prevailing rate of interest. And, so long as the banks go on progressively increasing their loans it will, therefore, be possible to continue the prolonged methods of production or perhaps even to extend them still further. But for obvious reasons the banks cannot continue indefinitely to extend credits; and even if they could, the other effects of a rapid and continuous rise of prices would, after a while, make it necessary to stop this process of inflation.[1]

Let us assume that for some time, perhaps a year or two, the banks, by keeping their rate of interest below the equilibrium rate, have expanded credit, and now find themselves compelled to stop further expansion. What will happen? (Perhaps it should be mentioned at this point that the processes I shall now describe are processes which would also take place if existing capital is encroached upon, or if, in a progressive society, after a temporary increase in saving, the rate should suddenly fall to its former level. Such cases, however, are probably quantitatively less important.)

Now we know from what has been said already that the immediate effect of the banks ceasing to add to their loans is that the absolute increase of the amount of money spent on consumers' goods is no longer compensated by a proportional increase in the demand for producers' goods. The demand for consumers' goods will for some time continue to increase because it will necessarily always lag somewhat behind

[1] For a fuller discussion of the reasons why this process of expansion must ultimately come to an end, whether the banks are restricted by reserve regulations, etc., or not, and of some of the points alluded to in the next paragraphs, see my article on "Capital and Industrial Fluctuations", *Econometrica*, April, 1934, p. 161.

the additional expenditure on investment which causes the increase of money incomes. The effects of such a change will, therefore, be similar to what would happen in the second case we have to consider, the case of an increase of money by consumers' credits. At this point, accordingly, the two cases can be covered by one discussion.

(8) Speaking generally, it might be said that the effects of a relative increase in the demand for consumers' goods are the reverse of the effects of an increase in the relative demand for producers' goods. There are, however, two important differences which make a detailed account necessary.

The first effect of the rise of the prices of consumers' goods is that the spread between them and the prices of the goods of the preceding stage becomes greater than the price margins in the higher stages of production. The greater profits to be obtained in this stage will cause producers' goods in use elsewhere which may be used in this stage to be transferred to it, and the all round increase of price margins between the stages of production which will follow will cause a widespread transfer of non-specific producers' goods to lower stages. The new demand for these goods will cause a relative rise of their prices, and this rise will tend to be considerable because, as we have seen, there will be a temporary rise in the price of consumers' goods, due to the transient discrepancy between demand and supply, greater than will be the case after the supply of consumers' goods has caught up with demand. These temporary scarcity prices of consumers' goods will, furthermore, have the effect that at first production will tend to shrink to fewer stages than will be necessary after equilibrium prices of consumers' goods have established themselves.

Very soon the relative rise of the prices of the original factors and the more mobile intermediate products will make the longer processes unprofitable. The first effect on these processes will be that the producers' goods of a more specific character, which have become relatively abundant by reason of the withdrawal of the complementary non-specific goods, will fall in price. The fall of the prices of these goods will make their production unprofitable; it will in consequence be discontinued. Although goods in later stages of production will generally be of a highly specific character, it may still pay to employ original factors to complete those that are nearly finished. But the fall in the price of intermediate products will be cumulative; and this will mean a fairly sudden stoppage of work in at least all the earlier stages of the longer processes.

But while the non-specific goods, in particular the services of workmen employed in those earlier stages, have thus been thrown out of use because their amount has proved insufficient and their prices too high for the profitable carrying through of the long processes of production, it is by no means certain that all those which can no longer be used in the old processes can immediately be absorbed in the short processes which are being expanded. Quite the contrary; the shorter processes will have to be started at the very beginning and will only *gradually* absorb all the available producers' goods as the product progresses towards consumption and as the necessary intermediate products come forward. So that, while, in the longer processes, productive operations cease almost as soon as the change in relative prices of specific and non-specific goods in favour of the latter and the rise of the rate of interest make them unprofitable, the released goods will find new employment only as the new shorter processes are approaching completion.[1] Moreover, the final adaptation will be further retarded by initial uncertainty as regards the methods of production which will ultimately prove profitable once the temporary scarcity of consumers' goods has disappeared. Entrepreneurs, quite rightly, will hesitate to make investments suited to this overshortened process, i.e., investments which would enable them to produce with relatively little capital and a relatively great quantity of the original means of production.

---

[1] The reason for this assymetry between a transition to longer processes of production, which need not bring about any of these peculiar disturbances, and a transition to shorter processes, which will regularly be accompanied by a crisis, will perhaps become more evident if it is considered that in the former case there will necessarily be time to amortize the capital invested in the existing structure before the new process is completed, while in the latter case this will evidently be impossible and therefore a loss of capital and a reduction of income inevitable. (In all these discussions it is assumed that technical knowledge remains the same; a shortening of the structure of production which is due to technical progress has an altogether different significance from that due to an increase of consumption.)

It seems something of a paradox that the self-same goods whose scarcity has been the cause of the crisis would become unsaleable as a consequence of the same crisis. But the fact is that when the growing demand for finished consumers' goods has taken away part of the non-specific producers' goods required, those remaining are no longer sufficient for the long processes, and the particular kinds of specific goods required for the processes which would just be long enough to employ the total quantity of those non-specific producers' goods do not yet exist. The situation would be similar to that of a people of an isolated island, if, after having partially constructed an enormous machine which was to provide them with all necessities, they found out that they had exhausted all their savings and available free capital before the new machine could turn out its product. They would then have no choice but to abandon temporarily the work on the new process and to devote all their labour to producing their daily food without any capital. Only after they had put themselves in a position in which new supplies of food were available could they proceed to attempt to get the new machinery into operation.[1] In the actual world, however, where the accumulation of capital has permitted a growth of population far beyond the number which could find employment without capital, as a general rule the single workman will not be able to

---

[1] *Cf.* the very similar example now given by C. Landauer, *Planwirtschaft und Verkehrswirtschaft*, 1931, p. 47.

produce enough for a living without the help of capital and he may, therefore, temporarily become unemployable. And the same will apply to all goods and services whose use requires the co-operation of other goods and services which, after a change in the structure of production of this kind, may not be available in the necessary quantity.

In this connection, as in so many others, we are forced to recognise the fundamental truth, so frequently neglected nowadays, that the machinery of capitalistic production will function smoothly only so long as we are satisfied to consume no more than that part of our total wealth which under the existing organisation of production is destined for current consumption. Every increase of consumption, if it is not to disturb production, requires previous new saving, even if the existing equipment with durable instruments of production should be sufficient for such an increase in output. If the increase of production is to be maintained continuously, it is necessary that the amounts of intermediate products in all stages is proportionately increased ; and these additional quantities of goods in process are of course no less capital than the durable instruments. The impression that the already existing capital structure would enable us to increase production almost indefinitely is a deception. Whatever engineers may tell us about the supposed immense unused capacity of the existing productive machinery, there is in fact no possibility of increasing production to such an extent. These engineers and also those economists who believe that we have more capital than we need, are deceived by the fact that many of the existing plant and machinery are adapted to a much greatei output than is actually produced. What they overlook is that durable means of production do not represent all the capital that is needed for an increase of output and that in order that the existing durable plants could be used to their full capacity it would be necessary to invest a great amount of other means of production in lengthy processes which would bear fruit only in a comparatively distant future. The existence of unused capacity is, therefore, by no means a proof that there exists an excess of capital and that consumption is insufficient : on the contrary, it is a symptom that we are unable to use the fixed plant to the full extent because the current demand for consumers' goods is too urgent to permit us to invest current productive services in the long processes for which (in consequence of " misdirections of capital ") the necessary durable equipment is available.

(9) Here then we have at last reached an explanation of how it comes about at certain times that some of the existing resources cannot be used, and how, in such circumstances, it is impossible to sell them at all— or, in the case of durable goods, only to sell them at very great loss. To provide an answer to this problem has always seemed to me to be the central task of any theory of industrial fluctuations ; and, though at the outset I refused to base my investigation on the assumption that unused resources exist, now that I have presented a tentative explanation of this

phenomenon, it seems worth while, rather than spending time filling up the picture of the cycle by elaborating the process of recovery, to devote the rest of this lecture to further discussion of certain important aspects of this problem. Now that we have accounted for the existence of unused resources, we may even go so far as to assume that their existence to a greater or lesser extent is the regular state of affairs save during a boom. And, if we do this, it is imperative to supplement our earlier investigation of the effects of a change in the amount of money in circulation on production, by applying our theory to such a situation. And this extension of our analysis is the more necessary since the existence of unused resources has very often been considered as the only fact which at all justifies an expansion of bank credit.

If the foregoing analysis is correct, it should be fairly clear that the granting of credit to consumers, which has recently been so strongly advocated as a cure for depression, would in fact have quite the contrary effect ; a relative increase of the demand for consumers' goods could only make matters worse. Matters are not quite so simple so far as the effects of credits granted for productive purposes are concerned. In theory it is at least possible that, during the acute stage of the crisis when the capitalistic structure of production tends to shrink more than will ultimately prove necessary, an expansion of producers' credits might have a wholesome effect. But this could only be the case if the quantity were so regulated as exactly to compensate for the initial, excessive rise of the relative prices of consumers' goods, and if arrangements could be made to withdraw the additional credits as these prices fall and the proportion between the supply of consumers' goods and the supply of intermediate products adapts itself to the proportion between the demand for these goods. And even these credits would do more harm than good if they made roundabout processes seem profitable which, even after the acute crisis had subsided, could not be kept up without the help of additional credits. Frankly, I do not see how the banks can ever be in a position to keep credit within these limits.

And, if we pass from the moment of actual crisis to the situation in the following depression, it is still more difficult to see what lasting good effects can come from credit-expansion. The thing which is needed to secure healthy conditions is the most speedy and complete adaptation possible of the structure of production to the proportion between the demand for consumers' goods and the demand for producers' goods as determined by voluntary saving and spending. If the proportion as determined by the voluntary decisions of individuals is distorted by the creation of artificial demand, it must mean that part of the available resources is again led into a wrong direction and a definite and lasting adjustment is again postponed. And, even if the absorption of the unemployed resources were to be quickened in this way, it would only mean that the seed would already be sown for new disturbances and new crises. The only way permanently to " mobilise " all available resources is, therefore, not to use artificial stimulants—whether during a crisis or thereafter—but to leave it to time to effect a permanent cure by the slow process of adapting the structure of production to the means available for capital purposes.

(10) And so, at the end of our analysis, we arrive at results which only confirm the old truth that we may perhaps prevent a crisis by checking expansion in time, but that we can do nothing to get out of it before its natural end, once it has come. In the next lecture I shall be dealing with some of the problems connected with a monetary policy suitable for the prevention of crises. Meanwhile, although so far our investigation has not produced a preventive for the recurrence of crises, it has, I hope, at least provided a guide to the maze of conflicting movements during the credit cycle which may prove useful for the diagnosis of the situation existing at any moment. If this is so, certain conclusions with regard to the methods commonly used in current statistical analysis of business fluctuations seem to follow immediately. The first is that our explanation of the different behaviour of the prices of specific and non-specific goods should help to substitute for the rough empirical classification of prices according to their sensitiveness, a classification based on more rational considerations. The second, that the average movements of general prices show us nothing of the really relevant facts ; indeed, the

index-numbers generally used will, as a general rule, fail even to attain their immediate object because, being for practical reasons almost exclusively based on prices of goods of a non-specific character, the data used are never random samples in the sense required by statistical method, but always a biased selection which can only give a picture of the peculiar movements of prices of goods of this class. And the third is that for similar reasons every attempt to find a statistical measure in the form of a general average of the total volume of production, or the total volume of trade, or general business activity, or whatever one may call it, will only result in veiling the really significant phenomena, the changes in the structure of production to which I have been drawing your attention in the last two lectures.

A NOTE ON THE HISTORY OF THE DOCTRINES DEVELOPED IN THE PRECEDING LECTURE

The central idea of the theory of the trade cycle which has been expounded in the preceding lecture is by no means new. That industrial fluctuations consist essentially in alternating expansions and contractions of the structure of capital equipment has often been emphasised. At one time, at the beginning of the second half of the last century, such theories even enjoyed considerable vogue and the financial journalists of those days frequently used a terminology which, intelligently interpreted, seems to imply essentially the same argument as that used here. The creation of " fictitious capital ", it was said, leads to the conversion of too much circulating into fixed capital which ultimately brings about a scarcity of disposable or floating capital which makes it impossible to continue or to complete the new undertakings and so causes the collapse. The reason why these theories did not prove more fruitful seems to have been that the concepts employed, particularly the concepts of the different kinds of capital, were too uncertain in their meaning to give a clear idea of what was really meant. But even if for this reason their popularity in the 'sixties and 'seventies was of a transient nature, they are of considerable interest as an expression of a fairly long and continuous strand of thought which occasionally came very near to modern ideas and in some instances leads very directly to some of the best known theories of today.

I have made no special study of the development of these doctrines (which they would well deserve) and I can therefore do no more than give a brief sketch of the main lines of development as I see them. It seems that all these doctrines trace back to Ricardo's doctrine of the conversion of circulating into fixed capital, developed in the chapter " On Machinery " in the third edition of his *Principles*. A relatively early attempt to apply these ideas to the explanation of crises was

made in 1839 by the American Condy Raguet.[1] But the
author who mainly developed and widely popularised it was
James Wilson, the first editor of the *Economist*.[2] It seems
to be from him that a host of English and French writers
adopted it.   In England it was particularly the group of
economists connected with the Manchester Statistical Society
who took up the idea.   Mr. T. S. Ashton in his recent Centenary
History of this Society[3] quotes several extremely interesting
extracts from lectures given to this society by T. H. Williams
in 1857 and John Mills in 1867 which show clearly the great
importance which they all attached to the " excessive con-
versions of floating into fixed capital " ; and he particularly
draws attention to a significant passage in W. St. Jevons'
early tract on the *Serious Fall in the Value of Gold*, published
in 1863 soon after he came to Manchester, where he says that
the remote cause of the commercial tides " seems to lie in the
*varying proportions which the capital devoted to permanent and
remote investment bears to that which is but temporarily invested
soon to reproduce itself.*"[4]   From the author who later on was
to be the first to provide the basis for that modern theory
of capital which now enables us to give more definite meaning
to these ideas, this statement is of special interest and makes
one wonder whether it may not be due to his early preoccupation with the problem of the trade cycle that he was
led to a correct appreciation of the rôle the time element
played in connection with capital.

A little later Bonamy Price developed these ideas in
considerable detail[5] and from him they were taken over in
France, where other authors like J. G. Courcelle-Seneuil

[1] Condy Raguet, *A Treatise on Currency and Banking*, London,
1839, p. 62 *et seq.*

[2] James Wilson, *Capital, Currency and Banking*, London, 1847,
articles XI, XIII and XVI, particularly p. 152 *et seq.* (articles
XI, XIII and XVII in the second edit. of 1859).

[3] T. S. Ashton, *Economic and Social Investigations in Manchester*,
1833-1933. *A Centenary History of the Manchester Statistical Society*,
London, 1934, p. 72 *et seq.*

[4] W. St. Jevons, *A Serious Fall in the Value of Gold Ascertained
and its Social Effects set Forth*, London, 1863, p. 10, in the reprint in
the *Investigations in Currency and Finance*, London, 1884, p. 28.

[5] Bonamy Price discussed these problems on numerous occasions.
Cf. however, particularly his *Chapters on Practical Political Economy*,
London, 1878, pp. 110-24.

and V. Bonnet[1] had been working on similar lines, by Yves Guyot, who not inappropriately summarised this theory by saying the " Commercial and financial crises are produced, not by over-production, but by over-consumption."[2]

In the German literature similar ideas were introduced mainly by the writings of Karl Marx. It is on Marx that M. v. Tougan-Baranovsky's work is based which in turn provided the starting point for the later work of Professor Spiethoff and Professor Cassel. The extent to which the theory developed in these lectures corresponds with that of the two last-named authors, particularly with that of Professor Spiethoff, need hardly be emphasised.

Another contemporary author who is evidently indebted to the same strand of thought and whose views on these problems are even more closely related to those taken in these lectures, but with whose work on this point I have unfortunately only became acquainted since he has collected his earlier scattered articles in book-form, is Professor C. Bresciani-Turroni. His monumental study of the German inflation (*Le Vicende del Marco Tedesco*, Milano, 1931) appears to me to be one of the most important contributions to the study of money which have appeared in recent years. Particularly the chapters on the influence of inflation on production and on the scarcity of capital after the stabilisation (Chapters 5 and 10, an abridged German version of the latter appeared in the *Wirtschaftstheorie der Gegenwart*, ed. by H. Mayer, vol. II, Vienna, 1931) seem to me of extraordinary interest and to contain a wealth of concrete illustrations of these difficult theoretical questions which is not to be found elsewhere. Few other foreign books on economic problems would equally deserve being made available in an English translation.

In view of the importance which so many theories of the trade cycle attach to the inter-relationships between the different forms of " capital " one might expect that investigations in this field should have received considerable help from the theory of capital. That this has hitherto been the case only to a very limited degree is mainly due to the rather unsatisfactory state

---

[1] On these authors, *cf.* E. v. Bergmann, *Geschichte der natio-nalökonomischen Krisentheorien*, Stuttgart, 1895, where the reader will find references to still further authors belonging to the same category.

[2] Yves Guyot, *La Science Économique*, English translation, *Principles of Social Economy*, London, 1884, p. 249.

of this theory which was mainly concerned with barren terminological debates or the question whether capital was to be regarded as a separate factor of production and how this factor was to be defined, instead of making its main task the general question of the *way* in which production was carried on. It would not be surprising if it would ultimately be that theory of the trade cycle, which consciously utilises the results of the only satisfactory theory of capital which we yet possess, that of Böhm-Bawerk, which should prove to be successful. It must be admitted, however, that, so far, the further elaboration of the ideas of Böhm-Bawerk, apart from two notable exceptions, have not helped us much further with the problems of the trade cycle. The two exceptions are Knut Wicksell and his pupil, Professor G. Åkerman. Particularly the difficult but important investigations in the *Realkapital und Kapitalzins* of the latter author (two parts, Stockholm, 1923 and 1924), which I did not yet know at the time when I wrote these lectures, seems to me to deserve particular attention as one of the few attempts to clear up the difficult problems which arise out of the existence of very durable capital goods.

It seems, however, not improbable that in the future the relationship between the theory of capital and the theory of the trade cycle may be reversed and that the former will be benefited by the progress of the latter. Only by studying the changes of the capitalistic structure of production will we learn to understand the factors which govern it, and it seems that the trade cycle is the most important manifestation of these changes. It is therefore not surprising that the study of the problems of the trade cycle should lead to the study of the theory of capital. As has been suggested before, this may have been the case with Jevons, and more recently it has certainly been true of Professor Spiethoff (*cf.* already his " Vorbemerkungen zu einer Theorie der Ueberproduktion ", *Schmollers Jahrbuch*, XXVI, 1902, particularly page 299 and his essay on " Die Lehre vom Kapital " in *Die Entwicklung der Deutschen Volkswirtschaft im* 19. *Jahrhundert*, vol. I, 1908).

THE CASE FOR AND AGAINST AN " ELASTIC "
CURRENCY

" The notion common . . . to 90 per cent. of the
writings of monetary cranks is that every batch of goods is
entitled to be born with a monetary label of equivalent value
round its neck, and to carry it round its neck until it dies."

D. H. ROBERTSON,
Economica, No. 23, June, 1928, p. 142.

(1) If the considerations brought forward in the
last lecture are at all correct, it would appear that the
reasons commonly advanced as a proof that the
quantity of the circulating medium should vary as
production increases or decreases are entirely un-
founded. It would appear rather that the fall of prices
proportionate to the increase in productivity, which
necessarily follows when, the amount of money remaining the same, production increases, is not only entirely
harmless, but is in fact the only means of avoiding
misdirections of production. So far as an increase of
production caused by a transition to more capitalistic
methods of production is concerned, this result bears
some resemblance to the theory underlying certain
proposals for stabilising the value of money so as to
keep, not the prices of consumers' goods, but incomes,
or the prices of the factors of production constant,

the prices of consumers' goods being allowed to fall as costs fall and *vice versa*.[1] Complete invariability of the effective money stream would, as we have seen, however, have the further effect that any transition to more capitalistic methods of production would also make a reduction of money income necessary, except in the case of complete vertical integration of production. This necessity, which in view of the notorious rigidity of wages is certainly very undesirable, could however only be avoided without causing misdirections of production, if it were possible to inject the required additional quantities of money in such a way into the economic system that the proportion between the demand for consumers' goods and the demand for producers' goods would not be affected. This is no doubt a task which cannot be solved in practice. But apart from the special difficulties which may arise from the existence of rigidities I believe that the conclusion stated above holds here not only for this case of the transition to more capitalistic methods of production but also for an increase of production caused by the absorption of unused resources. Furthermore, by another chain of reasoning —which is too long and complicated to reproduce here,

[1] That there is no harm in prices falling as productivity increases has been pointed out again and again, e.g. by A. Marshall, N. G. Pierson, W. Lexis, F. Y. Edgeworth, F. W. Taussig, L. Mises, A. C. Pigou, D. H. Robertson and G. Haberler. (For more detailed references see my article on " The ' Paradox ' of Saving ", *Economica*, May, 1931, p. 161.) *Cf.* also the stabilisation proposal made by Dr. Maurice Leven, mentioned by W. J. King in the *Journal of the American Statistical Association* of March, 1928, Supplement, p. 146, and the article by R. G. Hawtrey in the *Journal of the Royal Statistical Society*, vol. XCIII, Part I, 1930.

and which I have sketched elsewhere[1]—it might be shown to apply in principle even to the particularly difficult case of an increase of production caused by the growth of population, the discovery of new natural resources, and the like.   But however that may be, our result is in sufficient contrast to generally received opinions to require further elucidation.

(2) We can best observe how deeply the notion that it is the " natural " thing for the quantity of money to fluctuate with fluctuations in the volume of production is ingrained in the minds of many modern economists if we look at the use they make of it in their theoretical analysis. Professor Cassel, for instance, who is of course the outstanding representative of this point of view, discussing the treatment of price problems[2] in a recent article, writes as follows : " The simplest assumption is, then, that a country has a paper currency so regulated as to keep the general level of prices constant." And again—to quote another well-known authority—Professor Pigou is expressing the same opinion when he argues[3] that if countries with paper currencies will regulate them with a view to keeping the general price level in some sense stable, there will be no impulses from the side of money which can properly be called " autonomous ". Both statements imply that changes in the quantity

[1] In an article, " Das intertemporale Gleichgewichtssystem der Preise und die Bewegungen des ' Geldwertes ' ", *Weltwirtschaftliches Archiv*, vol. 28, July, 1928.

[2] *Economic Journal*, vol. 38, December, 1929, p. 589.

[3] *Industrial Fluctuations*, second edit., 1929, p. 101.

of the circulating medium which are only just sufficient to keep the general price level steady exert *no* active influence on the formation of prices, and that, accordingly, a money so regulated would remain " neutral " towards prices in the sense in which I have used the word. I see no foundation at all for this hypothesis, although by most it seems to be considered as an obvious platitude requiring no further justification. Everything that has been said in the earlier lectures seems to me to prove that changes in the volume of the circulation which are supposed to be justified by changes in the volume of production will have effects which are just as disturbing as those changes of the circulation which cause changes in the general price level. *Prima facie*, I suggest that we should expect rather that, to be neutral in this sense, the supply of money should be invariable. The question is, can this be true ? Are there not many other reasons besides a change in the volume of production which experience suggests justify changes in the quantity of money in circulation if serious disturbances are to be avoided ?

I suppose that, to most economists, the idea of a circulating medium which does not vary in amount will seem perfectly absurd. We have all been brought up upon the idea that an elastic currency is something highly to be desired, and it is considered a great achievement of modern monetary organisation, particularly of the recent American Federal Reserve system, to have secured it. It does not seem open to doubt that the amount of money necessary to carry on the trade of a country fluctuates regularly with the seasons, and that central banks should respond to these changes in the " demand for money ", that not only *can* they do this without doing harm, but that they *must* do so if they are not to cause serious disturbances. It is also a fact which has been established by long experience, that in times of crisis central banks should give increased accommodation and extend thereby their circulation in order to prevent panics, and that they can do it to a great extent without effects which are injurious. How are we to reconcile all this with the conclusions of my earlier lectures ?

(3) To begin with certain terminological elucidations. It should be fairly clear that the magnitude which in the course of my theoretical analysis I have called " quantity of money in circulation " and that commonly referred to under the same name in dealing with the practical problems mentioned before are not identical, but different in two respects. When, in the course of analysis, I speak of changes in the quantity of money, this is always meant to include that *total* of all kinds of media of exchange (including all so-called " substitutes " for money) used in either a *closed* economic system (i.e. in a country which has no communication with the outside world) or in the world as a whole. But when in dealing with practical problems we speak of the quantity of money in circulation, we always mean the quantity of any particular kind or kinds of media of exchange used within one or

several countries which form a part of a larger economic unit. Now, as we shall see, it follows from the definition of the quantity of money in circulation in open communities that the quantity of money thus defined will always be liable to fluctuations even if we suppose that the quantity included in the more comprehensive theoretical concept remains unchanged. It is probably this fact which makes it so difficult even theoretically to conceive the possibility or usefulness of an invariable circulation.

The fact that the monetary circulation of any one country, whatever we include under the heading money, will always show natural fluctuations in conforming with an increase or decrease of the volume of local production is probably the main reason why elasticity is generally considered a self-evident necessity for the amount of money in general. But the question we have to answer is just this. Do the reasons which make fluctuations of the circulation of *any single* country necessary apply when we are considering the quantity of money as a whole ?[1] The answer is simple. The increase or decrease of the quantity of money circulating within any one geographical area serves a function just as definite as the increase or decrease of ·the money incomes of particular individuals, namely the function of enabling the inhabitants to draw a larger or smaller share of the total product of the world. The relative magnitude of the total incomes of all individuals

[1] For a more detailed discussion of this problem, see my article in the *Weltwirtschaftliches Archiv* (vol. 28), quoted above, sect. 12.

in an " open " community will always stand in a
definite proportion to the share of the total product
of the world which the people of that community
command.   And, if the money circulating within that
nation regularly increases as a consequence of an
increase of its product, this is only one of the steps
in the process of adjustment which are necessary to
enable that nation to procure a larger portion of the
product of the world for itself.   What appears to be
an *absolute* increase of the amount of money in circulation consequent upon an increase of production, if
viewed from the standpoint of a single country, proves
to be nothing but a change in the *relative local distribution* of the money of all nations, which is a necessary
condition of a change in the distribution of the product
of the world as a whole.   The same thing would
happen, and would be just as necessary to restore
equilibrium, if the product of this country were not
absolutely increased but the products of all other
countries were absolutely diminished.   The fact that
the increase of the product of any one country is regularly accompanied by an increase of the quantity of
money circulating there, is therefore not only no proof
that the same would be necessary for an isolated
community, it rather shows by contrast how useless
would be an increase of its monetary circulation either
for such a community or for the world as a whole.
While for any single country among others an increase
of its possession of money is only a means of obtaining more goods, for the world as a whole the increase

of the amount of money only means that somebody has to give up part of his additional product to the producers of the new money.

(4) The second source of the prevalent belief that, in order to prevent dislocation, the quantity of the circulating medium must adapt itself to the changing needs of trade arises from a confusion between the demand for *particular kinds of currency* and the demand for money *in general*.[1] This occurs especially in connection with the so-called seasonal variations of the demand for currency which in fact arises because, at certain times of the year, a larger proportion of the total quantity of the circulating medium is required in *cash* than at other times. The regularly recurring increase of the " demand for money " at quarter days, for instance, which has played so great a rôle in discussions of central bank policy since attention was first drawn to it by the evidence of J. Horsley Palmer and J. W. Gilbart before the parliamentary committees of 1832 and 1841, is mainly a demand to exchange money held in the form of bank deposits into bank notes or coin.[2] The same thing is true in regard to the " increased demand for money " in the last stages of a boom and during a crisis. When, towards the end of a boom period, wages and retail prices rise, notes

[1] This confusion is particularly obvious in the writings of Thomas Tooke. *Cf.* T. E. Gregory, Introduction to Tooke and Newarch's *A History of Prices and the State of the Circulation*, London, 1928, p. 87 *et seq.*

[2] On this point, see, however, the recent discussion by F. Machlup, *Börsenkredit, Industriekredit und Kapitalbildung*, Vienna, 1931, particularly chaps. 8 and 9.

and coin will be used in proportionately greater amounts, and entrepreneurs will be compelled to draw a larger proportion of their bank deposits in cash than they used to do before. And when, in a serious crisis, confidence is shaken, and people resort to hoarding, this again only means that they will want to keep a part of their liquid resources in cash which they used to hold in bank money, etc. All this does not necessarily imply a change in the total quantity of the circulating medium, if only we make this concept comprehensive enough to comprise everything which serves as money, even if it does so only temporarily.

(5) But at this point we must take account of a new difficulty which makes this concept of the total quantity of the circulating medium somewhat vague, and which makes the possibility of ever actually fixing its magnitude highly questionable. There can be no doubt that besides the regular types of the circulating medium, such as coin, bank notes and bank deposits, which are generally recognised to be money or currency, and the quantity of which is regulated by some central authority or can at least be imagined to be so regulated, there exist still other forms of media of exchange which occasionally or permanently do the service of money. Now while for certain practical purposes we are accustomed to distinguish these forms of media of exchange from money proper as being mere substitutes for money, it is clear that, *ceteris paribus*, any increase or decrease of these money substitutes will have exactly the same effects as an increase or decrease

of the quantity of money proper, and should therefore, for the purposes of theoretical analysis, be counted as money.

In particular, it is necessary to take account of certain forms of credit not connected with banks which help, as is commonly said, to economise money, or to do the work for which, if they did not exist, money in the narrower sense of the word would be required. The criterion by which we may distinguish these circulating credits from other forms of credit which do not act as substitutes for money is that they give to somebody the means of purchasing goods without at the same time diminishing the money spending power of somebody else. This is most obviously the case when the creditor receives a bill of exchange which he may pass on in payment for other goods. It applies also to a number of other forms of commercial credit, as, for example, when book credit is simultaneously introduced in a number of successive stages of production in the place of cash payments, and so on. The characteristic peculiarity of these forms of credit is that they spring up without being subject to any central control, but once they have come into existence their convertibility into other forms of money must be possible if a collapse of credit is to be avoided. But it is important not to overlook the fact that these forms of credits owe their existence largely to the expectation that it will be possible to exchange them at the banks against other forms of money when necessary, and that, accordingly, they might never come into existence if people did not expect that the banks would in the future extend credit against them. The existence of this kind of demand for more money, too, is therefore no proof that the quantity of the circulating medium must fluctuate with the variations in the volume of production. It is only a proof that once additional money has come into existence in some form or other, *convertibility* into other forms must be possible.

(6) Before proceeding to investigate whether there exist any genuine reasons which would make changes in the amount of the circulation necessary in order to keep money entirely neutral towards the economic process (i.e., to prevent it from exercising any active influence on the formation of prices), it is useful to ask whether, under the circumstances just described, it is at all conceivable that the quantity of the circulating medium *can* be kept invariable, and by what means a monetary authority could attain that end. I may say at once that, in spite of the qualifications that I shall introduce later, this question seems to me not merely a question of theoretical interest, but also a question the answer to which may prove very important in the shaping of a more rational monetary policy.

The credit system of a country has very often been compared to an inverted pyramid, a simile which serves very well for our purpose. The lowest part of the pyramid corresponds of course to the cash basis of the credit structure. The section immediately above to central bank credit in its various forms, the next part to the credits of commercial banks, and on these finally is built the total of business credits outside the banks. Now it is only in regard to the two lower parts, cash and central bank credit, that an immediate control can be exercised by the central monetary authority. So far as the third part, the credits of the commercial banks, are concerned, it is at least conceivable that a similar control could be exercised. But the uppermost section of the pyramid—private credits—can be controlled only indirectly through a change in the magnitude of their basis, i.e., in the magnitude of bank credit. The essential thing is that the proportion between the different parts of the pyramid is not constant but variable, in other words that the angle at the apex of the pyramid may change. It is a well-known fact that, during a boom, the amount of central bank credits erected upon a given cash basis increases, and likewise the amount of credits of the commercial banks based on a given amount of central bank credit, and even the amount of private credits based on a given amount of central bank credit. This is certainly true on the continent of Europe, where the possibility of rediscounting takes to a large extent the place of actual cash reserves. So that, even if central banks should succeed in keeping the basis of the credit structure unchanged during an upward swing of a cycle, there can be no doubt that the total quantity of the circulating medium would none the less increase. To prevent expansion, therefore, it would not be sufficient if central banks, contrary to their present practice, refrained from *expanding* their own credits. To compensate for the change in the proportion between the base furnished by the credit and the superstructure erected upon it, it would be necessary for them actually to *contract* credit proportionally. It is probably entirely utopian to expect anything of that kind from central banks so long as general opinion still believes that it is the duty of central banks to accommodate trade and to expand credit as the increasing demands of trade require. Unfortunately, we are very far from the more enlightened times when, as John Fullarton complained, " the words ' demand ' and ' legitimate demand ' could not even be mentioned in Parliament in connection with this subject unaccompanied by a sneer ".[1] None the less, I am strongly convinced that, if we want to prevent the periodic misdirections of production caused by additional credit, something very similar to the policy outlined above, absurd as it may seem to those accustomed to present-day practice, would be necessary. I do not delude myself that, in the near future, there will be any opportunity of experimenting with such a policy. But this is no excuse for not following the implications of our theoretical arguments right through to their practical consequences. On the contrary, it is highly important that we should become fully conscious of the enormous difficulties of the problem of the elimination of disturbing monetary influences,

[1] John Fullarton, *On the Regulation of Currencies*, second edit., London, 1845, p. 206.

difficulties which monetary reformers are always so inclined to underrate. We are still very far from the point when either our theoretical knowledge or the education of the general public provide justification for revolutionary reform or hope of carrying such reforms to a successful conclusion.

(7) As a matter of fact, the course of our argument so far understates rather than overstates the real difficulties. I think that I have shown that changes in the physical volume of production offer no sufficient reason for variations in the supply of money. None the less there do seem to me to exist other causes whose operation may necessitate such changes if the "natural" price system or the equilibrium of the economic process is not to be disturbed. So far, I have been able to neglect these causes, since what I have said has been subject to an assumption, which I expressly introduced at the outset, the assumption, namely, that the proportion between the total flow of goods and the part which takes the form of an exchange against money, or the rate at which goods are exchanged against money, remains constant. But this assumption must now be removed.

Now it will be remembered that the proportion in question is not necessarily changed by changes in the physical volume of production while the amount of money in circulation remains the same, nor by a variation of the quantity of money in circulation, while the physical volume of production remains the same ; it changes only if movements of goods which before have been effected without the use of money now require the transfer of money, or if movements of goods which before could only be effected by means of money payments can now be effected without the use of money. It will be remembered further that changes in that proportion are caused by certain changes of the business organisation, as the amalgamation of two firms into one, or the division of one firm into two, by the extension of the money economy into spheres where before everybody had only consumed his own product, or where barter had predominated, and the like. The question to which we must now address our attention is this : Will not such changes in the proportions of money transactions to the total flow of goods make a corresponding change in the quantity of the circulating medium necessary ?

The answer to that question depends upon whether, without such a corresponding change in the quantity of money, the change in business organisation would cause shifts in the directions of demand and consequential shifts in the direction of production not justified by changes in the " real " factors. That the simple fact that a money payment is inserted at a point in the movement of goods from the original means of production to the final stage where none has been necessary before (or the reverse) is no " real " cause in the sense that it would justify a change in the structure of production, is a proposition which probably needs no further explanation. If, therefore, we can show that, without a corresponding change in the amount of the circulation, it has such an effect, this would provide sufficient reason, in these circumstances, to consider a change in the amount of money to be necessary.

(8) Let us examine what happens when a firm which represents two different stages of production, say spinning and weaving, is divided into two independent firms. The movement of the yarn from the spinning to the weaving factory, which before required no money, will now be effected by a purchase against money. The new weaving firm, which before, as part of the larger concern, had to keep money only for the payment of wages, etc., will now require additional money balances to buy the yarns. The new owner, whom we will assume to have bought the weaving mill from the old firm, will therefore need additional capital beyond what was needed to buy the existing plant and equipment and to replace the cash balances kept by the former owner for that mill, in order to effect these new payments. If no new money is added to the amount already circulating, he will either have to take this sum from other employments where it cannot be replaced, causing an absolute reduction of the demand for capital goods, and consequently a shrinkage of the structure of production ; or he will have to use new savings for that purpose, which would thus cease to be available for lengthening the roundabout processes—that is to say, to use a phrase of Mr. Robertson's, they would become " abortive ". The effects would be the same

as if, other things remaining the same, the total amount of money in circulation had been reduced by a corresponding sum used before for productive purposes. The two cases are so far alike that the change in the proportion between the demand for consumers' goods and the demand for producers' goods, which in the second case as in the first is not determined by " real " causes, will not be permanent: the old proportion will tend to re-establish itself. But if, from the outset, the demand of the new entrepreneur for the additional cash balances had been satisfied by the creation of new money, this change in the total quantity of circulation would not have caused a change in the direction of the demand, and would only have helped to preserve the existing equilibrium.

It would be easy to show, if time permitted, that in the contrary case, the merger of two firms, and in a number of similar changes in business organisation, money is set free and that this money, if not withdrawn from circulation, would have the same effects as if so much money were added to the circulation. But I think that what I have already said on this point will be sufficient to justify the conclusion that changes in the demand for money caused by changes in the proportion between the total flow of goods to that part of it which is effected by money, or, as we may tentatively call that proportion, of *the co-efficient of money transactions*, should be justified by changes in the volume of money if money is to remain neutral towards the price system and the structure of production.

All this assumes a greater importance if we remember that this co-efficient of money transactions may not only change in time, but that, at the same moment of time, it may be different in different parts of an economic system, for instance because goods change hands at shorter intervals in the lower stages of production than they do in the higher stages. If this is the case, any transfer of money from one part of the economic system to another or from one stage of production to another where the co-efficient of money transactions is different will also make a corresponding change of the amount of money in circulation necessary. If, for instance, money is transferred from a lower to a higher stage of production where the interval between two successive stages is twice as long, and, accordingly, only half as much money is needed to hold the same quantity of goods in that stage, half the money so transferred would become free. In the opposite case an addition of new money of an equal amount would be necessary. In such a situation, therefore, the transition to more or less capitalistic methods of production may also require a change in the quantity of money, *not* because the physical magnitude of the goods-stream has changed, but because money has been transferred from a sphere where the co-efficient of money transactions has been higher to one where it is lower, or *vice versa*.

(9) And this is not the only exception to which our original maxim of policy, that the quantity of money should remain invariable, may be deemed to be subject.

The case just discussed is, in fact, only a special aspect of a more general and very familiar phenomenon which so far has been entirely neglected in these lectures. I refer to changes in what is commonly called the velocity of circulation. Up to this point I have treated the quantity of money in circulation and the number of payments effected during a given period of time as equivalent concepts, a method of procedure which implied the assumption that the velocity of circulation is constant. That is to say, the whole of my argument applies directly only to the *amount of payments* made during a period of time. It applies indirectly to the *amount of money* if we assume the " velocity of circulation " to be constant. So long as we make that assumption, or so long as we are speaking only of the volume of payments made during a period of time, the case just discussed seems to me the only exception to the general rule that, in order that money should remain neutral towards prices, the amount of money or the amount of money payments should remain invariable. But the situation becomes different as soon as we take into account the possibility of changes in methods of payment which make it possible for a given amount of money to effect a larger or smaller number of payments during a period of time than before. Such a change in the " velocity of circulation " has rightly always been considered as equivalent to a change in the amount of money in circulation, and though, for reasons which it would go too far to explain here, I am not particularly enamoured of the concept of an average velocity of circulation[1] it will serve as sufficient justification of the general statement that any change in the velocity of circulation would have to be compensated by a reciprocal change in the amount of money in circulation if money is to remain neutral towards prices.

(10) Even now our difficulties are not at an end. For, in order to eliminate all monetary influences on the formation of prices and the structure of production, it would not be sufficient merely quantitatively to adapt the supply of money to these changes in demand, it would be necessary also to see that it came into the hands of those who actually require it, i.e., to that part of the system where that change in business organisation or the habits of payment had taken place. It is conceivable that this could be managed in the case of an increase of demand. It is clear that it would be still more difficult in the case of a reduction. But quite apart from this particular difficulty which, from the point of view of pure theory, may not prove insuperable, it should be clear that only to satisfy the legitimate demand for money in this sense, and otherwise to leave the amount of the circulation unchanged, can never be a practical maxim of currency policy. No doubt the statement as it stands only provides another, and probably clearer, formulation of the old distinction between the demand for additional money as money which is justifiable, and the demand for

[1] *Cf.* L. v. Mises, *Theorie des Geldes und der Umlaufsmittel*, second edit., München and Leipzig, 1924, p. 111 *et seq.*

additional money as capital which is not justifiable. But the difficulty of translating it into the language of practice still remains. The " natural" or equilibrium rate of interest which would exclude all demands for capital which exceed the real supply capital, is incapable of ascertainment, and, even if it were not, it would not be possible, in times of optimism, to prevent the growth of circulatory credit outside the banks.

Hence the only practical maxim for monetary policy to be derived from our considerations is probably the negative one that the simple fact of an increase of production and trade forms no justification for an expansion of credit, and that—save in an acute crisis—bankers need not be afraid to harm production by overcaution. Under existing conditions, to go beyond this is out of the question. In any case, it could be attempted only by a central monetary authority for the whole world : action on the part of a single country would be doomed to disaster. It is probably an illusion to suppose that we shall ever be able entirely to eliminate industrial fluctuations by means of monetary policy. The most we may hope for is that the growing information of the public may make it easier for central banks both to follow a cautious policy during the upward swing of the cycle, and so to mitigate the following depression, and to resist the well-meaning but dangerous proposals to fight depression by " a little inflation ".

(11) Anybody who is sceptical of the value of theoretical analysis if it does not result in practical suggestions for economic policy will probably be deeply disappointed by the small return of so prolonged an argument. I do not, however, think that effort spent in clearing up the conditions under which money would remain neutral towards the economic process is useless because these conditions will never be given in the real world. And I would claim for these investigations at least two things. The first is that, as I have said in my first lecture, monetary theory is still so very far from a state of perfection that even some of the most fundamental problems in this field are yet unsolved, that some of the accepted doctrines are of very doubtful validity. This applies in particular to the widespread illusion that we have simply to stabilise the value of money in order to eliminate all monetary influences on production and that, therefore, if the value of money is assumed to be stable, in theoretical analysis, we may treat money as non-existent. I hope to have shown that, under the existing conditions, money will always exert a determining influence on the course of economic events and that, therefore, no analysis of actual economic phenomena is complete if the rôle played by money is neglected. This means that we have definitely to give up the opinion which is still widely prevalent, that, in the words of John Stuart Mill, " there cannot, in short, be intrinsically a more insignificant thing, in the economy of society, than money " which " like many other kinds of

machinery only exerts a distinct and independent influence of its own when it gets out of order ".[1] It means also that the task of monetary theory is a much wider one than is commonly assumed ; that its task is nothing less than to cover a second time the whole field which is treated by pure theory under the assumption of barter, and to investigate what changes in the conclusions of pure theory are made necessary by the introduction of indirect exchange. The first step towards a solution of this problem is to release monetary theory from the bonds which a too narrow conception of its task has created.

The second conclusion to be drawn from the results of our considerations follows from the first : So long as we do not see more clearly about the most fundamental problems of monetary theory and so long as no agreement is reached on the essential theoretical questions, we are also not yet in a position drastically to reconstruct our monetary system, in particular to replace the semi-automatic gold standard by a more or less arbitrarily managed currency. Indeed, I am afraid that, in the present state of knowledge, the risks connected with such an attempt are much greater than the harm which is possibly done by the gold standard. I am not even convinced that a good deal of the harm which is just now generally ascribed to the gold standard will not by a future and better informed generation of economists be recognised

[1] J. S. Mill, *Principles of Political Economy*, Book III, Chap. VII, para. 3, ed. Ashley, p. 488.

as a result of the different attempts of recent years to make the mechanism of the gold standard inoperative. And there is still another and perhaps no less important reason why it seems dangerous to me to overstress at the present moment the urgency of a change in our monetary system ; it is the danger of diverting public attention from other and more pressing causes of our difficulties. I must say a last word on that point because it will help to prevent a misunderstanding which I am particularly anxious to avoid. Though I believe that recurring business depressions can only be explained by the operation of our monetary institutions, I do not believe that it is possible to explain in this way every stagnation of business. This applies in particular to the kind of prolonged depression through which some European countries are passing today. It would be easy to demonstrate by the same type of analysis which I have used in the last two lectures that certain kinds of State action, by causing a shift in demand from producers' goods to consumers' goods, may cause a continued shrinking of the capitalist structure of production, and therefore prolonged stagnation. This may be true of increased public expenditure in general or of particular forms of taxation or particular forms of public expenditure. In such cases, of course, no tampering with the monetary system can help. Only a radical revision of public policy can provide the remedy.

APPENDIX TO LECTURE IV

SOME SUPPLEMENTARY REMARKS ON "NEUTRAL MONEY"

The term "neutral money", as mentioned in Lecture I, was apparently first used by Wicksell, but more or less incidentally, and without the intention to introduce it as a technical term. It was only comparatively recently that it came to be more widely used, apparently first in Holland, probably owing to the influence of Mr. J. G. Koopmans, who has for years been investigating this problem. The first results of Mr. Koopmans' studies have, however, appeared only recently, since the present book was first published.[1] But Mr. Koopmans has carried his investigations considerably further than was possible in the present essay, and to anyone who is interested in that problem I can only warmly recommend Mr. Koopmans' study, with which I find myself in general agreement.

A short but earlier discussion of the problem is to be found in a German work by Mr. W. G. Behrens.[2] Mr. Behrens also points out correctly that this is only a new name for the problem which had been discussed by Carl Menger and Professor Mises under the, in my opinion rather unfortunate, name of the invariability of the " *innere objektive Tauschwert* " of money, or shortly of the " *innere Geldwert* ". And it may also be added that it was essentially for the same purpose that L. Walras and the later economists of the Lausanne School used the concept of a " *numeraire* " as distinguished from that of " *monnaie* ".

It is not intended here to go further into the extremely difficult theoretical problems which this concept raises. There is, however, one respect in which recent discussions devoted to it have shown a certain ambiguity of the concept, which it seems desirable to clear up. It is frequently assumed that the concept of neutrality provides a maxim which is immediately applicable to the practical problems of monetary policy.

[1] J. G. Koopmans, " Zum Problem des ' Neutralen ' Geldes ", in *Beiträge zur Geldtheorie*, ed. by F. A. Hayek, Vienna, 1933.

[2] Walter G. Behrens, *Das Geldschöpfungsproblem*, Jena, 1928, particularly pp. 228, 286, 312 *et seq.*

But this need by no means be the case, and the concept was certainly not primarily intended for that purpose. It was destined in the first instance to provide an instrument for theoretical analysis, and to help us to isolate the active influences, which money exercised on the course of economic life. It refers to the set of conditions, under which it would be *conceivable* that events in a monetary economy would take place, and particularly under which, in such an economy, relative prices would be formed, as if they were influenced only by the " real " factors which are taken into account in equilibrium economics. In this sense the term points, of course, only to a problem, and does not represent a solution. It is evident that such a solution would be of great importance for the questions of monetary policy. But it is not impossible that it represents only one ideal, which in practice competes with other important aims of monetary policy.

The necessary starting point for any attempt to answer the theoretical problem seems to me to be the recognition of the fact that the identity of demand and supply, which must necessarily exist in the case of barter, ceases to exist as soon as money becomes the intermediary of the exchange transactions. The problem then becomes one of isolating the one-sided effects of money—to repeat an expression which on an earlier occasion I had unconsciously borrowed from von Wieser,[1]— which will appear when, after the division of the barter transaction into two separate transactions, one of these takes place without the other complementary transaction. In this sense demand without corresponding supply, and supply without a corresponding demand, evidently seem to occur in the first instance when money is spent out of hoards (i.e., when cash balances are reduced), when money received is not immediately spent, when additional money comes on the market, or when money is destroyed. So this formulation of the problem leads immediately to the solution of a constant money stream, with the exceptions sketched in the last lecture. The argument has, however, been developed systematically only by Mr. J. G. Koopmans in the essay mentioned above.

In order to preserve, in the case of a money economy, the tendencies towards a stage of equilibrium which are described

[1] *Cf.* F. v. Wieser, " Der Geldwert und seine Veränderungen ", *Zeitschrift für Volkswirtschaft, Sozialpolitik und Verwaltung,* vol. XIII, 1904, p. 54, also reprinted in the same author's *Gesammelte Abhandlungen,* Tübingen, 1929, p. 178.

by general economic theory, it would be necessary to secure the existence of all the conditions, which the theory of neutral money has to establish. It is however very probable that this is practically impossible. It will be necessary to take into account the fact that the existence of a generally used medium of exchange will always lead to the existence of long-term contracts in terms of this medium of exchange, which will have been concluded in the expectation of a certain future price level. It may further be necessary to take into account the fact that many other prices possess a considerable degree of rigidity and will be particularly difficult to reduce. All these " frictions " which obstruct the smooth adaptation of the price system to changed conditions, which would be necessary if the money supply were to be kept neutral, are of course of the greatest importance for all practical problems of monetary policy. And it may be necessary to seek for a compromise between two aims which can be realised only alternatively : the greatest possible realisation of the forces working toward a state of equilibrium, and the avoidance of excessive frictional resistances. But it is important to realise fully that in this case the elimination of the active influences of money has ceased to be the only, or even a fully realisable, purpose of monetary policy ; and it could only cause confusion to describe this practical aim of monetary policy by the same name, which is used to designate the theoretically conceivable situation, in which one of the two competing aims was fully obtained.

The true relationship between the theoretical concept of neutral money, and the practical ideal of monetary policy is, therefore, that the former provides one criterion for judging the latter; the degree to which a concrete system approaches the condition of neutrality is one and perhaps the most important, but not the only criterion by which one has to judge the appropriateness of a given course of policy. It is quite conceivable that a distortion of relative prices and a misdirection of production by monetary influences could only be avoided if, *firstly*, the total money stream remained constant, and *secondly*, all prices were completely flexible, *and, thirdly*, all long term contracts were based on a correct anticipation of future price movements. This would mean that, if the second and third conditions are not given, the ideal could not be realised by any kind of monetary policy.

CAPITAL AND INDUSTRIAL FLUCTUATIONS

A Reply to a Criticism[1]

A SYMPATHETIC criticism of the kind to which the views of the present author have been subjected by Messrs. Hansen and Tout in a recent issue of *Econometrica*,[2] offers a welcome opportunity of clearing up some points upon which I have obviously not yet been sufficiently explicit. The critical comments of the two authors are mostly directed against points where real difficulties present themselves; and while I think I can answer their main objections, it is probable that I can do so more profitably by means of a further systematic development of my thesis than by wasting time on the comparatively unimportant discussion of whether these developments were already implied in my earlier statements, or whether the interpretation put upon these by Messrs. Hansen and Tout can, or cannot, be justified from the admittedly sketchy and incomplete exposition in the preceding lectures.

Messrs. Hansen and Tout have stated my theory in the following series of propositions:

Thesis Number 1. That depression is brought about by a shrinkage in the structure of production (i.e., a shortening of the capitalistic process). In Hayek's view, the phenomenon

[1] Reprinted from *Econometrica*, vol. ii., no. 2, April 1934.

[2] A. Hansen and H. Tout, " Annual Survey of Business Cycle Theory : Investment and Saving in Business Cycle Theory ", *Econometrica*, vol. i., no. 2, April 1933.

of depression *is* a shrinkage in the structure of production. Dynamic forces may bring about various effects on economic life, but unless they have the specific effect of shortening the process of production, depression will not follow therefrom. Nor does depression ever assume any other form than that of a shrinkage in the structure of production. In short, depression may be defined as a shortening of the capitalistic process of production.

Thesis Number 2. The leading cause (there are, however, others) which brings about, either directly or indirectly, a shortening in the process of production, is the phenomenon of *forced* saving.

Thesis Number 3. An elongation of the process of production caused by *voluntary* saving tends to remain intact; or at least, there is no inherent reason why such an elongation *must* necessarily be followed by a shrinkage in the structure of production.

An increase in voluntary saving would cause an enlarged demand for producers' goods in relation to consumers' goods, and this would raise the prices of goods in the higher stages of production in relation to those of the lower stages. The consequent narrowing of the price margins or, in other words, the lower rate of interest, would thus make possible a permanent elongation of the process of production.

Thesis Number 4. A lengthening of the process of production caused by forced saving (the money supply not having been held neutral) cannot possibly be permanently maintained, but must necessarily be followed by a shortening in the process of production.

An increase in money supply (bank credit) made available to entrepreneurs would cause an increase in the demand for producers' goods in relation to consumers' goods, and this would raise the prices of goods of the higher order in relation to those of the lower order. The consequent elongation of the process of production could not, however, be maintained, because a reversal in the price relationship of higher and lower order goods would appear as soon as the money supply ceased to increase owing to the fact that spending and saving habits had not changed. Thus, a shrinkage in the artificially elongated process of production would inevitably occur.

Thesis Number 5. An increase in consumer demand occasioned by an increase in the supply of money (over and above what may be necessary to hold money neutral) inevitably brings about a shortening in the process of production, and so causes depression.

An increased supply of money made available directly to consumers would cause an increase in the demand for consumers' goods in relation to producers' goods, and would thus raise the prices of goods of the lower order in relation to those of the higher order, and this would inevitably bring about a shortening in the process of production.

Thesis Number 6. That excessive public expenditures and taxation, by increasing the ratio of spending to saving, will force a shortening in the process of production and so cause prolonged depression or business stagnation.

An increase in spending would cause an increased demand for consumers' goods in relation to producers' goods, and this would raise the prices of goods in the lower order in relation to those of the higher order. The consequent widening of the price margins between the lower and higher order goods, or, in other words, a higher rate of interest, would, therefore, bring about a shortening of the process of production.

Thesis Number 7. That the supply of money should be kept constant, except for such increases and decreases as may be necessary (1) to offset changes in the velocity of circulation, (2) to counteract such changes in the co-efficient of money transactions as are occasioned by the amalgamation of firms, and the like, and (3) to provide for any changes in non-monetary means of payment, such as book credit, that may be taking place. (A distinction is thus made between a " constant " money supply and a " neutral " money supply.)

Thesis Number 8. That any change in money supply (other than that necessary to hold money neutral) is harmful because it necessarily brings about, eventually, a shortening in the process of production. (a) If the increased money supply goes to entrepreneurs, the process of production is first elongated, but, subsequently, necessarily shortened, returning to its previous status, or to a still shorter process. (b) If the increased money goes first to consumers, the shortening of the process of production takes place at once, and the process remains permanently shortened.

Thesis Number 9. That an increase in production and trade forms no justification for an increase in bank credit.

Thesis Number 10. That a period of depression should not be counteracted by any inflation of the money supply, though, in theory, there is the possibility that during the acute stages of the crisis, while the capitalistic structure is tending to shrink more than will ultimately prove necessary, a nicely regulated increase might prove beneficial. The impossibility of such skilful management makes this an unimportant exception.

I

With one exception, I fully agree that this formulation of my views is a fair and accurate summary of my position. Even the unimportant exception is probably only a slip of the pen, and is satisfactorily cleared up in the later discussion. But, as it may have confused some readers, I should like to emphasise at the outset that I should never say, as stated in thesis number 2 that forced saving can ever *directly* bring about a shortening of the process of production. Forced saving means essentially a lengthening of the process of production and the crucial point is that, in my view, it is these elongations which are likely to be partly or wholly *reversed* as soon as the cause of the forced saving *disappears*.

The first major difficulty which Messrs. Hansen and Tout discuss, is connected with what they call my thesis number 1, namely, that the phenomenon of depression is equivalent to a shrinkage of the structure of production. Their difficulty here seems to me to turn on the distinction between a completed and an uncompleted structure, which I have probably failed to make sufficiently clear, and which is closely connected with the distinction between the effects of mere fluctuations in the rate of saving (or, more correctly, in the rate of investment) and the peculiar instability of capital created by means of forced saving. The best way of making these distinctions clear is probably to start with a general discussion of the effects of fluctuations in the means available for investment on the structure of production in general, and on the profitableness of the early stages in particular. From this discussion it will, I think, appear that, contrary to the opinion of Messrs. Hansen and Tout, it is not the mere fluctuations in the rate of investment which tend to make the earlier stages unprofitable but only, on the one hand, particularly violent fluctuations of this sort, and, on the other, fluctuations which make the net investment negative. Finally, concluding this part of the discussion, it will appear that, in the case of " forced savings ", it is not only impossible to keep the rate of investment constant, but that there will exist, as a necessary consequence of the " forced saving ", strong forces which tend to make the rate of investment negative.

II

Any lengthening of the process of production can only be completed over a period of time corresponding to the interval between the moment when the factors which are being shifted to an earlier stage are being invested, and the moment when their product matures. If the new, longer process is to be completed and maintained, this requires not only that the investment in the earlier stage must be constantly maintained, but also (except in a few rare cases, like the ageing of wine and the growing of trees) that further complementary investments must be made in the later stages.

From this it follows that, in any progressive society, the particular forms in which investments are being made are determined by the expectation that, for some time to come, a similar stream of funds for investment will be forthcoming ; and that, at any moment of time, only a fraction of the funds available for new investment will be used to start new processes, while the rest will be required to complete the processes already under way.   On the simplifying assumption that the *total* length of the marginal processes which are made possible by an increase in the supply of investible funds, is always greater than the total length of any process already used, this situation can be represented by the following diagram. The curvilinear[1] triangle ABC represents, in the same way as the triangle I have used in the preceding lectures, the stock of capital belonging to processes already completed. (The area of the curvilinear triangle $AB'C'$ shows the stock of capital before the additions were begun.) The fully drawn stripes, beginning between C and D, represent incomplete processes, started at different moments in the past —and now in different stages of completion. The part of these stripes which is dotted represents the

[1] The reasons which make a curvilinear triangle of the kind shown in the text a more appropriate representation than the simplified form used in Lecture II are probably obvious. See p, 39.

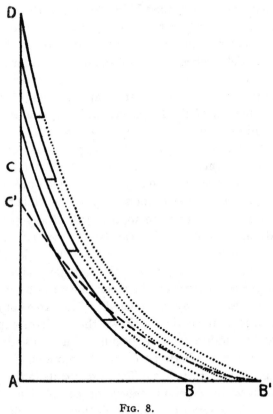

FIG. 8.

additional investment which is required to complete the processes. During every successive period of investment, part of the fund available will be used to start new processes, part to advance processes which are already under way, and part to complete the most advanced processes.

If at any moment savings fall by no more than had previously been used to start new processes, the completion of the processes already under way will not be endangered. And since, at any moment, some of the unfinished processes will be completed, the amount of saving may continually fall off at a certain rate, and may reach zero at the moment when all the processes under way are completed. There is, therefore, at any moment, a maximum rate at which the rate of saving may fall off, without interfering with the new processes already started. It is only when the decrease in saving is faster than this rate, at which the need for capital for the purpose of completing processes under way decreases, that the incomplete structure cannot be completed and some of the investments made in the earlier stages have to be abandoned.

Such an abandonment of early stages will, of course, mean that the average period for which the current supply of original factors is being invested, is shortened even if, at the same time, a good deal of investment in new forms in later stages is taking place. In this case, however, investment in new forms need *not* mean *net* investment, since the losses on the abandoned earlier stages have to be offset against it.

III

It is only another way of stating the same conclusions if one says that the total demand for producers' goods will fall off in consequence of a decrease in the demand for new producers' goods only if the latter declines faster than the replacement demand increases, in consequence of the preceding growth of the stock of producers' goods. And this brings me to a discussion of the famous argument according to which any increase in the demand for productive equipment must lead to surplus capacity of plant producing that equipment, as soon as the demand for it ceases to increase. Although this is rarely recognised, this is a typical instance where an expansion of an earlier stage of production can be maintained only if the further increase of capital makes it possible to complete the structure by adequate increases of capital in the later stages.[1]

From the very outset, it is important in this connection carefully to avoid a confusion which arises from the failure to distinguish between fluctuations in the demand for productive equipment of a particular industry, which arise from fluctuations in the demand for the product of that industry, and fluctuations in the demand for new producers' goods in general, which are connected

[1] A top-heavy structure of this kind is, therefore, an uncompleted structure in the sense that its earlier stages will be permanently employed only after they have helped to increase the equipment in later stages to such a magnitude that its replacement demand will fully use the capacity of the earlier stages. (The essential thing here, however, is not capacity in a technical sense, but sufficient employment to make amortisation of plant at current prices possible.)

with fluctuations in the supply of funds available for new investment. Here I am mainly concerned with the latter type of fluctuation. How far what is to be said about this particular case is also applicable to the former, depends upon the degree to which the concrete capital equipment in earlier stages is specialised to the production of equipment for a particular industry, or whether it can be more generally used. On this question of fact, I can only refer to an interesting article which was recently published by Mr. Seltzer,[1] who seems to show that the mobility of capital in this sense is far greater than is commonly supposed. Some other considerations on this point can be more appropriately discussed after I have dealt with the first type of fluctuation.

At first, therefore, I shall assume that the increase in investment is due to an increase in the supply of capital, and that the plant required to provide the new equipment is not adapted to the requirements of one industry only, but can be used fairly widely. The question then is whether, on the expectation of a continued growth of capital at about the same rate, it will appear profitable to expand the plant in the industries producing that equipment to a point where *any* decline in the current supply of new capital will make full use of that plant unprofitable.

The answer to this question is simply this: as long as the supply of capital does not decrease by more than the

[1] "The Mobility of Capital", *Quarterly Journal of Economics*, vol. 46, 1932.

amount which has so far been used to construct the new plant[1] making that equipment, there is no reason why the demand for new equipment should fall off. In other words, the effect of a decrease in saving will simply be that the beginning of new roundabout processes will be stopped but, if the decrease does not exceed a certain rate, there is no reason why the already existing plant should not be continuously used to add to the equipment in later stages. And as the replacement demand due to earlier additions to this equipment will continue to rise, the supply of new savings may even continue to fall at a certain rate without affecting the employment of the plant producing this equipment. The situation is, therefore, completely analogous to the case of fluctuations in the rate of saving already

---

[1] It is assumed here that the construction of this additional plant for making the equipment in question can be carried out either with the help of similar plant already in existence, or of some other plant which can *also* be used to produce equipment for later stages. This, of course, will always be the case since no capital is created without the help of some capital already in existence, which if it is a question of adding an earlier stage of production to those already existing, must, *ex definitione*, mean that these capital goods have hitherto been used in later stages. It may be mentioned here, since this has occasionally been a cause of confusion, that any given capital good need not, and usually will not, belong to any one given " stage " of production only. If it is used to produce other capital goods employed in different stages, and still more if it helps to produce durable goods, or is itself durable, it belongs to as many different " stages " as different periods of time elapse from the moment in which we consider it, to the moments when the different final products which it has helped to produce are consumed. This, however, so far from making the concept of stages useless, is only a necessary distinction in order to explain the different ways in which the value of individual capital goods will be affected by changes in the supply of capital, the rate of interest, or other factors affecting the structure of production.

discussed : it need not have any harmful effects, so long as the decline in the rate of saving does not exceed the amount, which will permit the processes already begun to be completed.

IV

The confusion on this point seems to result from a very common mistake—that of applying what is true of a single industry to industry as a whole. While, of course, the relative magnitude of the demand for equipment for a particular industry will depend upon the demand for the product of that industry, it is certainly not true to say that the demand for capital goods in general is directly determined by the magnitude of the demand for consumers' goods. While it is true that some contemporary economists have come so much under the influence of the under-consumptionist fallacy that they are prepared to say that the savings will never lead to a corresponding increase in investment, because they involve a decline in the demand for consumers' goods, and are therefore only a harmful and undesirable phenomenon, I certainly need not discuss this with economists who accept as much of my fundamental position as do Messrs. Hansen and Tout. But, if one accepts the proposition that the magnitude of the total demand for producers' goods is not a simple derivative of the demand for consumers' goods, but that any given demand for consumers' goods can lead to methods of production involving very different demands for producers' goods, and that the particular method of production chosen will depend upon the proportion of the total wealth *not* required for immediate consumption, then we must certainly take the fluctuations in the supply of free capital, and not the fluctuations in the demand for consumers' goods, as the starting point for this kind of analysis.

There is, therefore, no reason to suppose that a general increase in the demand for new capital goods, which is due to an increase in the supply of saving, must lead to a decrease in the demand for capital goods, as soon as the rate of saving begins to decline. And since I am still abstracting from the case where investment is financed by the creation of credit (" forced saving ") or any other purely monetary changes, it is difficult to see what factors can affect the *total* demand for new capital goods, other than the supply of savings. Only if we assume that changes in the rate of interest which can be earned on new capital lead to hoarding or dishoarding, would a new cause of change be introduced. But this is one of the cases of monetary changes in the demand for consumers' goods which I shall have to discuss later on.

On this point, my argument so far amounts to this : that in so far as we abstract from monetary changes, the demand for consumers' goods can only change inversely with the demand for producers' goods, and in consequence, so far from having a cumulative effect in the same direction as the latter, will tend to offset it in the opposite direction.

There is, however, still the case of mere shifts of demand between different kinds of consumers' goods which, of course, will have some effect on the demand for particular kinds of capital goods. An unexpected shift of this kind will undoubtedly have the effect that provision made for the supply of new equipment in the industry from which demand has turned away, will now prove excessive or, in other words, it will now become unprofitable to complete the longer processes in the expected way. But the total demand for new equipment will not be changed, and whether the equipment-producing plant already in existence will continue to be used or whether new plant will have to be built, will depend upon the technical considerations already mentioned.

V

So much for the pure, or barter, theory of the subject (in the sense of the usual assumption of theory that money exists to facilitate exchange but exercises no determining influence on the course of things, or, in other words, remains neutral—an assumption which is almost always made though not expressed in these terms). The discussion of the active influence which may be exercised by money in this connection is best begun with the peculiar effect of forced savings, which will lead us to another of the points of discussion, namely, the effect of monetary changes on the demand for consumers' goods. For the peculiar characteristic of forced saving, which distinguishes its effects from those of voluntary saving, is simply that it leads necessarily to an increase in the means available for the purchase of consumers' goods. For this reason, my thesis number 4 about the impermanence of capital accumulated by forced saving is directly bound up with my thesis number 5 as to the effects of a direct increase in the monetary demand for consumers' goods, which Messrs. Hansen and Tout, quite consistently, also reject.

The reason why forced saving will always lead to a subsequent increase in the money available for the purchase of consumers' goods, is fairly obvious and will probably not be contested. Entrepreneurs are in this case enabled to attract factors of production from later to earlier stages, not by a corresponding transfer of funds from consumers' to producers' goods, but by additional money handed to them. This means that they will bid up the prices of these factors without there being a corresponding fall in the prices of other factors. Total money income will therefore increase, and this increase will in turn lead to an increase in the amount of money expended on consumers' goods. This increase in the expenditure on consumers' goods will necessarily follow in time upon the increase in the demand for factors. This lag will mean that, for some time after the demand for factors (or producers' goods) has ceased to increase (or when its rate of increase begins to slow down), the demand for consumers' goods will continue to increase at a faster rate ; and so long as the increase in the demand for producers' goods is slowing down—and for some time afterwards—the monetary proportion between the demand for producers' goods and the demand for consumers' goods will change in favour of the latter.

The question turns, therefore, upon the effect of such a relative increase in the monetary demand for consumers' goods. The reply, in the particular case in question, however, is simplified, in comparison with the general problem, because, on our assumptions, two relevant points are given. We have in this particular case to assume that : (a) since it is the situation at the end of a boom, there are no unemployed resources, and (b) since the rate of credit expansion for productive purposes tends to be slowed down in spite of a continued rise in the monetary demand for consumers' goods, we cannot assume that the continued rise in this demand will lead to a renewed credit expansion. The much more difficult case of an increase in the monetary demand for consumers' goods, where these assumptions do not necessarily hold, as well as the problem why the rate of credit expansion cannot be sufficiently high to avoid this type of reaction, will be considered later on.

The relative rise in the price of consumers' goods will not only improve the competitive position of their producers on the market for original factors, but will also make it profitable for these to increase their output by the more rapid, even if more expensive, method of employing relatively more labour (original factors) in proportion to capital. And while their demand for all the non-specific factors of production (which can also be used in the latest stages of production) will continue to drive up the prices of these factors, the prices of the intermediate products specific to earlier stages of production will tend to fall relatively to their costs. And since the effect of this will not only tend to increase cumulatively towards the earlier stages but will also cause a shift of free capital towards the more profitable earlier stages, it is easy to see how more and more of the earlier stages will tend to become unprofitable, until unemployment finally arises and leads to a fall in the prices of the original factors of production as well as in the prices of consumers' goods.

VI

Before I turn to the aspects of the situation where unemployed factors and unused lending capacity of all banks exist, and where, perhaps, delay in making the necessary adjustments has led to prolonged unprofitability causing deflation and a rapid general fall of prices, a little more must be said about the rate of credit expansion which would have to continue uninterruptedly if a reaction of the kind just discussed is to be avoided.

Messrs. Hansen and Tout merely speak of a *steady* rate of credit expansion as a sufficient condition for a continuous and undisturbed rate of capital growth. I am not quite sure what " steady " means in this context. But if it refers, as is probably the case, to a constant rate of increase in the total media of circulation, I think it can be shown that this is not sufficient to maintain a constant rate of forced saving; while it seems that any attempt to make the rate of credit expansion great enough to secure a constant rate of forced saving will inevitably be frustrated by counteracting forces which come into operation as soon as the process of inflation exceeds a certain speed.

A constant rate of forced saving (i.e., investment in excess of voluntary saving) requires a rate of credit expansion which will enable the producers of intermediate products, during each successive unit of time, to compete successfully with the producers of consumers' goods[1] for constant additional quantities of the original factors of production. But as the competing demand from the producers of consumers' goods rises (in terms of money) in consequence of, and in proportion to, the preceding increase of expenditure on the factors of production (income), an increase of credit which is to enable the producers of intermediate products to attract additional original factors, will have to be, not only absolutely but even relatively, greater than the last increase which is now reflected in the increased demand for consumers' goods. Even in order to attract

---

[1] I am compelled here—as I was in the preceding lecture—to speak, for the sake of brevity, in terms of competition between the producers of intermediate products and the producers of consumers' goods (the present and future goods of Böhm-Bawerk's exposition) instead of speaking more correctly of competition between a continuous range of entrepreneurs in all " stages " of production, which leads to all original factors being invested for a shorter or longer average period.

only as great a proportion of the original factors, i.e., in order merely to maintain the already existing capital, every new increase would have to be proportional to the last increase, i.e., credit would have to expand progressively at a constant *rate*. But in order to bring about constant additions to capital, it would have to do more : it would have to increase at a *constantly increasing rate*. The rate at which this rate of increase must increase would be dependent upon the time lag between the first expenditure of the additional money on the factors of production and the re-expenditure of the income so created on consumers' goods.

It is true that in the preceding lectures I have not only discussed in detail what rate of credit expansion is required to maintain a given rate of forced saving, but have simply assumed that that rate—whatever it was—could not be permanently maintained for institutional reasons, such as traditional banking policies or the operation of the gold standard. But I think it can be shown without great difficulty that even if these obstacles to credit expansion were absent, such a policy would, sooner or later, inevitably lead to a rapid and progressive rise in prices which, in addition to its other undesirable effects, would set up movements which would soon counteract, and finally more than offset, the " forced saving ".

That it is impossible, either for a simple progressive increase of credit which only helps to maintain, and does not add to, the already existing " forced saving ", or for an increase in credit at an increasing rate, to continue for a considerable time without causing a rise in prices, results from the fact that in neither case have we reason to assume that the increase in the supply of consumers' goods will keep pace with the increase in the flow of money coming on to the market for consumers' goods. In so far as, in the second case, the credit expansion leads to an ultimate increase in the output of consumers' goods, this increase will lag considerably and increasingly (as the period of production increases) behind the increase in the demand for them. But whether the prices of consumers' goods will rise faster or slower, all other prices, and particularly the prices of the original factors of production, will rise even faster. It is only a question of time when this general and progressive rise of prices becomes very rapid. My argument is not that such a development is *inevitable* once a policy of credit expansion is embarked upon, but that it *has to be* carried to that point if a certain result—a constant rate of forced saving, or maintenance without the help of voluntary saving of capital accumulated by forced saving—is to be achieved.

Once this stage is reached, such a policy will soon begin to defeat its own ends. While the mechanism of forced saving continues to operate, the general rise in prices will make it increasingly more difficult, and finally practically impossible, for entrepreneurs to maintain their existing capital intact. Paper profits will be computed and consumed, the failure to reproduce the existing capital will become quantitatively more and more important, and will finally exceed the additions made by forced saving.

It is important in this connection to remember that the entrepreneur necessarily and inevitably thinks of his capital in terms of money, and that, under changing conditions, he has no other way of thinking of its quantity than in value terms, which practically means in terms of money. But even if, for a time, he resists the temptation of paper profits (and experience teaches us that this is extremely unlikely) and computes his costs in terms of some index number, the rate of depreciation has only to become fast enough, and such an expedient will be ineffective. And since the gist of my argument is that, for the purpose under discussion, the rate of credit expansion and depreciation has to increase at an increasing rate, it will in time reach any desired magnitude.

VII

For these reasons, it seems to me that the hope of Messrs. Hansen and Tout based on a steady rate of forced saving is illusory. Whether there may not exist conditions under which temporary forced saving may take place without the evil consequences of a crisis, is quite another matter. That this will be possible only if the rate of forced saving is comparatively small, is probably obvious. Another condition which we already know is that the fluctuations in investment to which it gives rise keep well within the limits we have described.   In another place,[1] I have tried to show that, if these conditions are combined with a third, namely, the presence of a relatively high rate of voluntary saving, which provides the means of taking over, as it were, the real capital which has been created but cannot be maintained by means of forced saving, the loss of this capital may be avoided.   But in this case, the only one I know where such a loss will be avoided, the forced saving will only mean an anticipation but no net increase of the circulation of capital, because it can only be maintained if an equivalent amount of saving is to be forthcoming later.   For this reason, I am even more doubtful than before whether forced saving can ever be a blessing as Messrs. Hansen and Tout think. This is quite irrespective of the question whether there is any sense in which the economist can legitimately say (as I have occasionally said myself) that such decisions made against the will of those concerned may be " beneficial ".   But that touches the much wider problem of whether we possess any gauge by which to measure the satisfaction derived by those concerned, except their own preferences, shown in their decisions— a question which I cannot even begin to discuss here.

VIII

It will be impossible within the compass of this article to discuss the further points made by Messrs. Hansen and Tout in the same orbit as those more

[1] " Stand und Zukunftsaufgaben der Konjunkturforschung ", *Festschrift für Arthur Spiethoff*, p. 110.

fundamental problems already taken up.   Particularly, the next and very important point as to the effect of an expansion of consumers' demand at a time when the productive forces are not fully employed, and banks are in a position to expand credits to producers, could be answered completely only in connection with a fully developed theory of the process going on during a depression.   But, if it be assumed that these two conditions exist as a consequence of a preceding crisis (and a definite assumption as regards the reason *why* these conditions exist is essential for any answer), and if the explanation of the crisis which I have just discussed is accepted, it is difficult to see how the same phenomenon, which has brought about the crisis, i.e., the rise in the relative demand for consumers' goods, should also be the cure for it.   The scarcity of capital, which, of course, is nothing else but the relatively high price of consumers' goods, could only be enhanced by giving the consumers more money to spend on final products.   At least so long as there are no further monetary complications, particularly so long as it is not assumed that the expectation of a further fall in prices has led to hoarding, I see no way of getting over this difficulty.   But before I proceed to the relation between these secondary monetary complications, and the underlying real maladjustments which have caused it, I must try to clear away what seems to me to be a confusion which has led Messrs. Hansen and Tout to apply their denial of the capital-destroying effect of additions to consumers' credits, not only to the peculiar situation of an advanced depression, but also generally.

The essence of the confusion on this point seems to me to lie in the contrast which my critics try to establish in several places between what they call " nominal " changes in the relative monetary demand for consumers' goods and producers' goods, and the " real changes in the demand for consumers' goods occasioned by a fundamental modification in time preference for present and future goods ". It seems to me that, to assume that this rate of time preference can have any effect other than through the relative demand for these two classes of goods, or can have any immediate effects different from those of any other cause affecting that relative demand, is an attempt to establish a purely mystical connection. The mere fact that, even without a monetary change, any change in the distribution of the command over existing resources will, under a given set of individual time preferences, lead to quite different proportions between capital and income, should suffice to make this quite clear.[1]

---

[1] This fact is partly realised by the authors who, however, seem to underestimate its importance, mainly because they think only of the effects of a change in the distribution of *income ;* and while this is obviously the only factor which will affect *new savings*, the total supply of free capital depends even more on turnover or amortisation of existing capital. Any change in that stock of existing capital, brought about by monetary causes, will, by means of the consequent redistribution of the command over resources, tend to affect the relative demand for producers' and consumers' goods. If the monetary causes have led to a destruction of capital, this change will necessarily be permanent. If they have led to the creation of additional capital goods, the effect on relative demand *may* be, at least to some extent, permanently to increase the relative demand for capital goods.

Nor can I see how the two authors can combine their acceptance of the idea that forced saving can be brought about by monetary causes, without a change in the rate of time preference, with a general denial that monetary causes may also lead to " forced dis-saving ". In principle, any change in the relative demand for the two categories of goods, whether brought about by actual shifts of monetary demand from one to the other, or merely by unilateral increases or decreases without corresponding changes on the other side, will *tend* to lead to corresponding changes in the relative amounts produced. The differences between these two cases (a shift and a unilateral change) are, *first* that the shift of an amount of money from the demand for consumers' goods to the demand for producers' goods changes the proportion between the two much more effectively than a mere unilateral increase or decrease by the same amount ; and, *second*, that the changes in the quantity of money, which are implied in the second type of change, will lead to further changes which may counteract or offset the tendency created by the change in relative demand. This will be particularly true if a change in relative demand is accompanied by an absolute reduction in demand and if, at the same time, costs (i.e., the prices of the original factors of production) are rigid. In this case, deflationary tendencies are likely to set in, which may more than counter-balance the effect of the changed relative demand. But, in spite of these further complications which seem likely to arise, the principle seems to me to be true, and to comprise even what seems to Messrs. Hansen and Tout a *reductio ad absurdum* of the argument, namely that a unilateral decrease in the demand for consumers' goods may lead to a lengthening of the structure of production. Although I fully admit that, because of the probable complications, this case is very unlikely to materialise, I do not think that it is entirely imprac- tical. Would Messrs. Hansen and Tout deny that, e.g., increased hoarding on the part of a class of very small rentiers who reduced their consumption of agricultural products, might not lead, via the reduction of wages, first in agriculture and then generally, to an increase in the real quantity of labour corresponding to a constant amount of money invested in industry, and therefore of capital ?

IX

The analysis of this and similar cases would help to bring out an important distinction which Messrs. Hansen and Tout tend to overlook : the distinction between the tendencies set up directly by a given monetary change, and the effects of the further mone- tary changes which may, and perhaps even probably will, but need not, be induced by this first change. A sharp dividing line is the more necessary here since the tendency in current discussions is either to take these secondary monetary changes for granted, without ever mentioning them, or to fail to demonstrate why, and under what conditions, they should follow the first change.

These considerations bring me back to the problem of the relation between the demand for consumers' goods and the prices of capital goods. I should not deny that there may be conditions where, e.g., the expectation of a general price fall has led to extensive hoarding, and where any change in this expectation may lead to such dishoarding of funds available for investment as to outbalance the initial effect of the increase in the demand for consumers' goods.[1] Nor is it inconceivable that a similar situation may prevail as regards bank lending. There can also be no doubt that, in connection with these secondary monetary complications, *general* price movements, apart from the changes in relative prices, will be of the greatest importance, and that anything which stops or reverses the general price movement may lead to induced monetary changes, the effect of which on the demand for consumers' goods, and producers' goods, may be stronger than the initial change in the quantity of money.

But one has to be careful not to fall into the error apparently made by Messrs. Hansen and Tout—that of assuming that, in all cases, where the prices of consumers' goods and producers' goods move in the same direction (e.g., upwards), this may not be accompanied by changes in their relative height, which would produce exactly the same effect as if there were no general price movement. Their general proposition that changes in the relative prices of consumers' goods

[1] *Cf.* my contribution to the *Festschrift für Arthur Spiethoff,* quoted above.

and producers' goods will not have the same effect when they are accompanied by a universal movement in the same direction as when they find expression in an absolute movement in different direction, is only true under the following assumptions : (1) that the expected general price movement is relatively great compared with the relative price changes; (2) that, at the same time, the general movement does not exceed the limits beyond which—as experience has shown at least in cases of considerable inflation—costs begin to move more rapidly than prices; (3) that money rates of interest do not adapt themselves to the expected rate of general price change.[1]

Further, it is necessary to be careful to make clear the special assumptions under which these further complications are likely to arise. The deflationary

---

[1] It is a curious fact that the discussion of the supposedly different effect of changes in the relative demand which are due to changes in the supply of money leads the two authors to argue—in effect, if not explicitly, and on what seems to me to be wrong grounds—what they had previously denied, namely that capital accumulated by means of " forced saving " will not be permanent. If it were true that when, after a change in the supply of money, " equilibrium is finally established, the relation (between the prices of consumers' goods and the prices of producers' goods) will be found unaltered unless the effects of the transition period have been such as to change permanently the time preference of the income receivers " (p. 143), then, no doubt, the greater part of the real capital created by means of forced saving would be lost. But I think it will be clear by now why I should be very reluctant to use this argument in defence of my position.

Messrs. Hansen and Tout think that such a permanent change in the time preference of the income receivers " is not unlikely, since an increase or decrease in money supply is likely to increase the real income of the community ". This seems to show conclusively that what they have in mind is not the effect on the quantity and distribution of resources, but on individual time preferences.

tendencies, which are assumed to exist in most of the reasoning of the kind discussed, are not a necessary consequence of any crisis and depression, but are probably due to resistances to the necessary readjustments, caused by rigidity of prices, the existence of long term contracts, etc., I am far from underrating the importance of these phenomena. What I am pleading for is only that, for analytical purposes, these tendencies should carefully be kept separate and not confused with one another. Only in this way can we hope ultimately to unravel the tangle of different forces at work during a depression, and to arrive at that detailed explanation of the depression which I cannot even attempt here. But to deny the existence of certain tendencies merely because they are likely to be counteracted by others, does not seem to me to be a promising procedure.

X

The objections raised by Messrs. Hansen and Tout to what they call my theses 7, 8, 9, and 10, are partly based on arguments which I have already discussed and partly introduce further complications which any programme of practical policy has to face and which I admit I have not investigated sufficiently. But it is obviously impossible to develop my ideas further, in this connection, or to try to make good these deficiencies here.

There are only two more points upon which I wish to touch. The first is that the concept of neutral money was meant in the first place to be an instrument of theoretical analysis and not necessarily a tool of practical policy. Its purpose was to bring out clearly the conditions under which we could expect the economic process in a money economy to correspond perfectly to the picture drawn by the theory of equilibrium and, incidentally, to show what we should have to consider as the peculiar active effects caused by monetary changes. In a sense, of course, this would also set up an ideal of policy. But it is by no means inconceivable that considerations other than the direct monetary influences on prices, such as the existence of long term contracts in fixed sums of money, the rigidity of prices, and such like institutional factors, may make such an attempt entirely impracticable, because it would set up frictions of a new kind. In that case, the task of monetary policy would be to find a workable compromise between the different incompatible aims. But, in this case, one would have to be clear that certain important determining and disturbing influences arising from monetary causes would remain in existence, and that we should always have to remain conscious of this fact. Or, in other words, that even under the best practicable monetary system, the self-equilibrating mechanism of prices might be seriously disturbed by monetary causes.

The second point is that up to 1927 I should, indeed, have expected that because, during the preceding boom period, prices did not rise—but rather tended to fall—the subsequent depression would be very mild.

But, as is well known, in that year an entirely unprecedented action was taken by the American monetary authorities, which makes it impossible to compare the effects of the boom on the subsequent depression with any previous experience. The authorities succeeded, by means of an easy-money policy, inaugurated as soon as the symptoms of an impending reaction were noticed, in prolonging the boom for two years beyond what would otherwise have been its natural end. And when the crisis finally occurred, for almost two more years, deliberate attempts were made to prevent, by all conceivable means, the normal process of liquidation. It seems to me that these facts have had a far greater influence on the character of the depression than the developments up to 1927, which from all we know, might instead have led to a comparatively mild depression in and after 1927.